Anecdotes of the late
SAMUEL JOHNSON, LL.D.

The Summer House at Streatham

Anecdotes of the late SAMUEL JOHNSON, LL.D., during the last twenty years of his Life. By Hesther Lynch Piozzi

Edited, with an Introduction, by S. C. ROBERTS

CAMBRIDGE
AT THE UNIVERSITY PRESS
MCMXXV

CAMBRIDGE
UNIVERSITY PRESS

University Printing House, Cambridge CB2 8BS, United Kingdom

Cambridge University Press is part of the University of Cambridge.

It furthers the University's mission by disseminating knowledge in the pursuit of education, learning and research at the highest international levels of excellence.

www.cambridge.org
Information on this title: www.cambridge.org/9781316619971

© Cambridge University Press 1925

First published 1925
First paperback edition 2016

A catalogue record for this publication is available from the British Library

ISBN 978-1-316-61997-1 Paperback

CONTENTS

FRONTISPIECE

THE SUMMER HOUSE AT STREATHAM

(From an engraving by E. Finden after a drawing by C. Stanfield, R.A.)

PREFACE

A WORK relating to Samuel Johnson, which was printed four times in the year of publication, surely deserves a reprint at a time when there is a marked renewal of interest in *Johnsoniana*.

In a short *Introduction* I have tried not to propound new theories, but to summarise some of the evidence available for a proper judgment upon the relations between Johnson and the Streatham household. Whether charmed or exasperated by Mrs Thrale, students of Johnson cannot afford wholly to neglect her.

I must add that for the suggestion of this new edition and for much help in its preparation I am indebted to Mr Andrew Gow.

S. C. R.

CAMBRIDGE
31 *December* 1924

BIBLIOGRAPHY

No attempt has been made to catalogue either Mrs Thrale's contributions to periodical literature or the many references to her in that literature. The object of this bibliography is rather to give a chronological list of the principal works written by, or about, Mrs Thrale. An account of Mrs Thrale's writings will be found in the *Introduction* (pp. xxxvii ff.).

Miscellanies in Prose and Verse. By Anna Williams. London, 1766.

> Mrs Thrale's poem *The Three Warnings* appeared first in this collection.

The Florence Miscellany. Florence, 1785.

> Mrs Thrale contributed the Preface, several poems, and the Conclusion. *The Arno Miscellany*, published in the previous year, is described in the British Museum catalogue as "edited by Mrs Thrale," but does not appear to contain any contribution by her.

Anecdotes of the late Samuel Johnson, LL.D. during the last twenty years of his life. By Hesther Lynch Piozzi. London, 1786.

> The second, third, and fourth editions appeared in the same year, also one printed at Dublin. New editions were printed in 1822 and 1826.
>
> Croker "incorporated with the text nearly the whole of Mrs Piozzi's *Anecdotes*" in his notorious edition of Boswell's *Life* (1831). In the edition of 1835 they appear in a separate volume of *Johnsoniana*.
>
> The *Anecdotes* were reprinted in the Traveller's Library (1856) and in Cassell's National Library (1886).
>
> They are also included in the volume of *Johnsoniana* which forms part of Napier's edition of Boswell's *Life* (1884) and in Birkbeck Hill's *Johnsonian Miscellanies* (1897).

Bozzy and Piozzi, or, the British Biographers, a Town Eclogue. By Peter Pindar, Esq. London, 1786.

> A satire by John Wolcot. See p. xli.

Letters to and from the late Samuel Johnson, LL.D. To which are added Some Poems never before printed. Published from the original MSS in her possession, By Hester Lynch Piozzi. In two volumes. London, 1788.

> A Dublin edition was published in the same year.
>
> Birkbeck Hill's edition of the *Letters of Samuel Johnson* (two volumes, 1892) includes the letters written by Johnson.

Observations and Reflections made in the course of a journey through France, Italy, and Germany. By Hester Lynch Piozzi. In two volumes. London, 1789.

> A Dublin edition appeared in the same year and a German translation of selections, edited by G. Forster, in 1790.

The Three Warnings, A Tale. By Mrs Thrale. Kidderminster, 1792.

> There is a copy of this edition in the University Library, Cambridge. The poem is reprinted by Hayward (II, 165).

British Synonymy; or, an attempt at regulating the choice of words in familiar conversation. Inscribed, with Sentiments of Gratitude and Respect, to such of her Foreign Friends as have made English literature their peculiar Study, by Hester Lynch Piozzi. In two volumes. London, 1794.

> An abridged edition, with additional notes, was published in Paris in 1804.

Retrospection: or A Review of the most striking and important events, characters, situations, and their consequences, which the last eighteen hundred years have presented to the view of mankind. By Hester Lynch Piozzi. With a portrait of the Author. In two volumes. London, 1801.

Piozziana; or Recollections of the late Mrs Piozzi. With remarks. By A Friend. London, 1833.

> The friend is the Rev. E. Mangin, who was intimate with Mrs Piozzi at Bath in the last years of her life.

Diary and Letters of Madame D'Arblay, Author of *Evelina, Cecilia* &c. Edited by her niece. In 7 volumes. London, 1842.

> New editions appeared in 1854, in 1890–1 (with notes by W. C. Ward), and in 1904–5 (ed. A. Dobson). The period 1778–84 is largely occupied with Fanny Burney's account of life at Streatham. See p. xxv.

Love Letters of Mrs Piozzi, written when she was eighty, to William Augustus Conway. London, 1843.

Autobiography Letters and Literary Remains of Mrs Piozzi (Thrale). Edited with notes and an introductory account of her life and writings. By A. Hayward, Esq., Q.C. In two volumes. London, 1861.

> A second and enlarged edition, to which references are here given, appeared in the same year.
>
> These volumes contain most of what is at present available of Mrs Thrale's autobiographical work and the second edition includes more than the first.
>
> Hayward's material consisted of (1) Autobiographical Memoirs, (2) Letters, mostly addressed to Sir James Fellowes, (3) Fugitive pieces, many of them not previously printed, (4) MS notes on her own and other published works. Hayward was only supplied with extracts from *Thraliana*, the diary kept by Mrs Thrale from 1776 to 1809. This MS, which was also used by the late Mr Charles Hughes (see below), is now in the Huntington Library, and has never been printed in its entirety. The arrangement of Hayward's volumes is so bad as to make them almost unreadable as a continuous narrative.

Mrs Thrale afterwards Mrs Piozzi. A sketch of her life and passages from her diaries, letters, & other writings. Edited by L. B. Seeley, M.A. London, 1891.

> A new edition appeared in 1908. Based chiefly on Hayward.

Glimpses of Italian Society in the Eighteenth Century. From the Journey of Mrs Piozzi. With an Introduction by the Countess Évelyn Martinengo Cesaresco. London, 1892.

> Extracts from the *Observations and Reflections* with an Introduction on Mrs Piozzi's continental travels.

Doctor Johnson and the Fair Sex. A Study of Contrasts. By W. H. Craig, M.A., of Lincoln's Inn. London, 1895.

> For Dr Johnson and Mrs Thrale, see pp. 49–69.

Dr Johnson's Mrs Thrale. Autobiography, Letters and Literary Remains of Mrs Piozzi. edited by A. Hayward, Q.C. Newly selected and edited with introduction and notes by J. H. Lobban. 1909.

> A much-needed attempt to put Hayward's material in proper order (see Mr Lobban's *Preface*).

Doctor Johnson and Mrs Thrale: including Mrs Thrale's unpublished Journal of the Welsh Tour made in 1774 and much hitherto unpublished correspondence of the Streatham coterie. By A. M. Broadley with an introductory essay by Thomas Seccombe. London, 1910.

> As the title-page indicates, much new and valuable material is contained in this book and the introductory essay includes a vigorous defence of Mrs Thrale.

Mrs Piozzi's Thraliana with numerous extracts hitherto unpublished. By Charles Hughes. London, 1913.

> Mr Hughes had the good fortune to be lent the MS of *Thraliana*, but printed only a very few extracts (see *Introduction*, p. xxiii).

The Intimate Letters of Hester Piozzi and Penelope Pennington 1788–1821. Edited by Oswald G. Knapp. London, 1914.

> Letters to Penelope Weston, afterwards Mrs Pennington. The letters are supplemented by a connecting narrative.

INTRODUCTION

I N the long catalogue of *Johnsoniana*, no volume has aroused more controversy than the *Anecdotes* of Mrs Piozzi. Did Mrs Thrale cultivate Johnson as a literary lion while her husband lived and afterwards show him that he was not wanted? Or, on the other hand, did Johnson presume too far upon his friendship with Thrale and attempt to exercise an intolerable tyranny over his widow? It is doubtful whether the truth can be found in a categorical answer to either question. Certainly the material for even a partial answer must be sought in an appreciation of Mrs Thrale and the Streatham *milieu*.

⟨. *Mrs Thrale, afterwards Mrs Piozzi*

Hester Lynch Salusbury, the daughter of the 'rakish' John Salusbury of Bachygraig, was born 16 January 1741 at Bodvel in Carnarvonshire. She was, she says, the joint plaything of her parents and, "although education was a word then unknown as applied to females," she was taught to read and speak and think and translate from the French until she was "half a prodigy." Famous people petted her at an early age; she sat on Garrick's knee and was taught by Quin to recite passages from *Paradise Lost*.

While her father continued his rakish career in Nova Scotia under the patronage of Lord Halifax, "quarrelling and fighting and fretting his friends at home," Hester and her mother lived with relatives—first with "Grandmamma Cotton" at East Hyde, near Luton, and afterwards with her uncle, Sir Thomas Salusbury, at Offley Place. At East Hyde the girl learned to love horses: "When my mother hoped I was gaining health by the fresh air, I was kicking my heels on a corn binn, and learning to drive of the old coachman." Study, however, was equally delightful to her, and from the age of thirteen she was instructed in Latin, logic, rhetoric and other subjects by her dear Dr Collier, afterwards the preceptor of Sophy Streatfield.

Suitors for Miss Salusbury's hand came quickly. Each one of them was made to understand her extraordinary value: "Those who could read were shown my verses; those who could not were judges of my prowess in the field."

One of the disappointed suitors lived to be master of a Cambridge college. This was Dr James Marriott, at that time a lawyer of Doctors Commons and afterwards Master of Trinity Hall. John Salusbury's treatment of Dr Marriott as a possible son-in-law was in the true Squire Western manner:

Should you continue to insult my poor child...I shall take the Insult to myself; be then most certainly assured that I will be avenged on you, much to the detriment of your person. So help me God[1].

One day Sir Thomas Salusbury (now a widower

[1] Quoted in Broadley, *Doctor Johnson and Mrs Thrale*, p. 105.

and himself planning a second marriage) returned from London with news of a suitor of exceptional eligibility, "an incomparable young man...a model of perfection, and a *real sportsman*." When the young man arrived in person, he began, after the manner of wise suitors, by paying compliments to the mother—and with good effect: "There was little doubt of her approving the pretensions of so very showy a suitor." But Hester herself received no such favourable impression: "Nothing resembled love *less* than Mr Thrale's behaviour"; and her father was almost as violent in his opposition to the new suitor as he had been against the unfortunate Dr Marriott. He would not, he swore, have his daughter exchanged for a barrel of porter.

Under these doubtful auspices did Henry Thrale enter Hester Salusbury's life; but the situation was changed by the sudden death of John Salusbury in 1762. Ten months later Mr Thrale accepted what his bride declares to have been her undesired hand.

Born in 1728, Henry Thrale was the son of Ralph Thrale, the wealthy Southwark brewer. His education had been that which befitted an eighteenth-century gentleman—Eton, Oxford, the grand tour with a Lyttelton as companion. His allowance after he left college, says Boswell (perhaps with a touch of envy), was splendid—not less than a thousand a year. Probably it was an allowance which Henry Thrale, a gay man of the town and the boon companion of Arthur Murphy, was quite capable of spending. At the age of thirty he succeeded his father as head of the brewery. No wonder that he should appear to Sir Thomas Salusbury as a paragon amongst suitors. To a person of keener sensibility the only ground of offence was his occupation. He had offered his hand and his fortune to several ladies before he came to Offley Place, but all had refused to live in the Borough. *Nonne olet?* was the attitude of the more fastidious.

The story of Mrs Thrale's married life is a curious one. From the familiar passage in Boswell we receive an impression of a scholarly gentleman, an able man of business, a good husband and father who kept a quietly firm hand upon a somewhat frivolous wife:

Johnson had a very sincere esteem for Mr Thrale, as a man of excellent principles, a good scholar, well skilled in trade, of a sound understanding, and of manners such as presented the character of a plain independent English Squire....'I know no man (said he) who is more master of his wife and family than Thrale. If he but holds up a finger, he is obeyed....'

Side by side with this there may be quoted part of the *Character of Thrale*, of remarkable but characteristic objectivity, written by his wife:

Mr Thrale's person is manly, his countenance agreeable, his eyes steady and of the deepest blue; his look neither soft nor severe, neither sprightly nor gloomy, but thoughtful and intelligent; his address is neither caressive nor repulsive, but unaffectedly civil and decorous; and his manner more completely free from every kind of trick or particularity than I ever saw any person's....Mr Thrale's sobriety, and the decency of his conversation, being wholly free from all oaths, ribaldry and profaneness, make him a man exceedingly comfortable to live with; while the easiness of his temper and slowness to take offence add greatly to his value as a domestic man. Yet I think his servants do not much love him, and I am not sure that his children have much affection for him....With regard to his wife, though little tender of her person, he is very partial to her understanding; but he is obliging to nobody, and confers a favour less pleasing than many a man refuses to confer one. This appears to me to be as just a character as can be given of the man with whom I have now lived thirteen years....

Neither winter in Southwark nor summer in Streatham held at first any attraction for the young bride who had all her life been a spoilt child. Her place, in her husband's view, was either in the drawing-room or the bed-chamber. A pack of hounds was kept, but it was "masculine" to ride; the Streatham table was famous for its profusion, but Thrale would not have his wife *think of the kitchen*.

Certain members of Henry Thrale's acquaintance were introduced to the bride at Streatham; among them were Arthur Murphy, the 'facetious' Georgey Bodens, Simon Luttrell and Dr Fitzpatrick, "a very sickly old physician." Lacking her husband's confidence and discouraged by her mother from plunging into social gaiety, Mrs Thrale had to be content with her books and her

children. Still, this period of seclusion ("shut from
the world, its pleasures or its cares"), about which
Mrs Thrale writes with somewhat insistent self-
pity, did not last for long. Johnson was introduced
by Arthur Murphy in 1765; the fox-hounds were
sold; a seat in Parliament for Henry Thrale was
talked of; Mrs Thrale began to feel herself grow
useful, '*almost* necessary.'

Gradually the Thrale household gained a celebrity which is a matter not of controversy, but of
social history. Not only did Mrs Thrale become
famous, in Wraxall's words, as "the provider and
conductress of Dr Johnson," but her *salon* could
vie with those of the most distinguished blue-
stockings. Mrs Vesey, indeed, "dreamed not of
any competition, but Mrs Montague and Mrs
Thrale were set up as rival candidates for colloquial
eminence and each of them thought the other alone
worthy to be her peer." Clearly, Mrs Thrale was
something more than a successful lion-hunter.
While she was willing to let her lions roar, she was
herself a personality in conversation. The wife of
a Member of Parliament, she had both the ability
and the income necessary for successful entertaining, and she had also a genuine taste for letters.
The entrance into her life of Murphy, Johnson,
the Burneys and the others who followed gave her
exactly what she needed for the display of her
social talent. Her guests were not likely to be
squeamish—as the young ladies are said to have

been—either about Henry Thrale's occupation or about his residence in the Borough. Whether at Southwark or at Streatham they enjoyed good dinners and vivacious conversation. Boswell, though notoriously jealous of the hold which Mrs Thrale obtained over Johnson, was as keen as the rest to enjoy the hospitality of Streatham, not only because he realised that a successful *Life* of Johnson must include Streatham in its orbit, but because Mrs Thrale was herself a centre of social celebrity. That, in itself, was a sufficient attraction for James Boswell.

As for Johnson, there can be no doubt of the genuineness of his affection both for the Thrales individually and for the Streatham household collectively. He travelled with them in France and in Wales, stayed with them in Brighton as well as in London and, in particular, took a very serious interest in the business of brewing. In commerce Thrale appears to have been a man of one ambition —to outbrew Whitbread. Johnson, with characteristic readiness to interest himself in affairs of which he had no personal experience, enjoyed playing the rôle of consultant. "We are not far," he wrote on 23 August 1777, "from the great year of a hundred thousand barrels, which, if three shillings be gained upon each barrel, will bring us fifteen thousand pounds a year...."

Similarly in the matter of Thrale's digestion— and on this matter he might claim to speak with greater authority—Johnson issued his dietary injunctions with brotherly sternness:

If Mr Thrale at all remits his vigilance, let the Doctor loose upon him While he is watched he may be kept from mischief, but he never can be safe without a rule....

If Mr Thrale eats but half his usual quantity, he can hardly eat too much. It were better however to have some rule....

The rule to which Johnson refers was one of 'alternate diet'[1] to which he had repeatedly challenged his friend. But Thrale disregarded the warnings. The final seizure occurred in April 1781. Johnson had declared that Thrale's voracity was little better than suicide. Thrale replied by inquiring when the lamprey season would come in, and in this royal manner he died.

After her husband's death Mrs Thrale's immediate problems were concerned with her children, her brewery, and Dr Johnson. Between Mrs Thrale and her daughters (her only son had died) there was, to say the least of it, a lack of sympathy[2]; as to the brewery, the story of the negotiations for its sale is told in some fulness in the *Letters to and from Samuel Johnson* and in the extracts from *Thraliana* quoted by Hayward; the

[1] Birkbeck Hill conjectures that this meant abstention from animal food every other day (*Letters*, II, 143).

[2] The antagonism was, of course, most evident in the matter of the Piozzi marriage. Baretti has much to say, in his *Strictures* (*vide* p. xlii), of Mrs Thrale's treatment of her daughters.

Letters may also be taken as a fair guide to the relations between the widow and Dr Johnson.

It was not until the marriage with Piozzi became imminent that the bitter attacks began. Leaving aside, for the moment, the somewhat wearisome minutiae of the controversy, there can be no doubt that in the main Mrs Piozzi cheated the prophets. She married Piozzi because she loved him and it was a happy marriage. Piozzi was very different from the dashing foreigner of fiction who carries off his bride in a whirlwind of passion and subsequently breaks her heart with cruelty, infidelity, and extravagance. When the Piozzis returned from their wedding-tour, the Streatham house was not immediately given up. It had been let for several years, but on 28 July 1790 Mrs Piozzi wrote: "We have kept our seventh wedding day and celebrated our return to *this house* with prodigious splendour and gaiety. Seventy people…" and while the full glory of the Johnson period could scarcely be revived, Mrs Piozzi was very far from being a social outcast. Arthur Murphy, Dr Lort, Sir Lucas Pepys, Mrs Siddons and many others renewed their former friendships and Dr Parr wrote her "very flattering" letters. But Streatham Park was expensive, and after a few years Piozzi resolved to build an Italian villa on the banks of the Clwydd. A musician of simple tastes, Gabriel Piozzi was a man who, in spite of unfamiliarity with the English language, settled down comfortably to the life of a country gentleman at Brynbella. He repaired the village church and built a new vault for his wife's ancestors; he provided the cottagers with warm rugs for the winter; at the same time he showed a certain shrewdness in domestic finance, remarking that "white monies were good for ladies, yellow for gentlemen." He "conformed to English religious opinions" and became English even in his ailments, being "so punished with gout," that he was obliged to spend the winters at Bath.

It was at Bath that Mrs Piozzi's last years were spent. Widowed a second time in 1809, she moved there five years later. From various sources we get glimpses of the old lady's persistent liveliness. Tom Moore was taken to call upon her in 1819: "A wonderful old lady; faces of other times seemed to crowd over her as she sat—the Johnsons, Reynoldses, etc., etc.: though turned eighty, she has all the quickness and intelligence of a gay young woman."

On her eightieth birthday she sent more than six hundred invitations to a Concert, Ball, and Supper in the Bath Assembly Rooms. "The Dancing commenced at two when Mrs Piozzi led off with Sir J. Salusbury[1] and proved to the company that the season of infirmity was yet far distant." A few months later, however, infirmity was hastened by a travelling accident, and in May 1821 Mrs Piozzi died.

[1] Her adopted son.

❰ *The Streatham Circle*

In an extract from *Thraliana* quoted by the late Mr Hughes[1] there is reproduced part of "a most remarkable tabular character sketch of the society of Streatham, based on a system of marks for different quantities, 20 being full marks." Unfortunately Mr Hughes, who had the rare opportunity of reading the whole of *Thraliana*, omitted some of the records of the men[2], and all those of the ladies, who belonged to the Streatham circle; but, even so, the mark-sheet, with its nine columns headed respectively Religion, Morality, Scholarship, General Knowledge, Person and Voice, Manners, Wit, Humour, Good Humour[3] has many points of interest:

Johnson, for instance, gets full marks for Religion, Morality, and General Knowledge, 19 for Scholarship, 16 for Humour, 15 for Wit, and nothing at all for the three remaining subjects; Murphy scores about 75 per cent. for all subjects except Religion, Morality, and General Knowledge, for which his marks are very low; Burney has high marks for everything except Scholarship, Wit, and Humour; Garrick's average

[1] *Mrs Piozzi's Thraliana,* by Charles Hughes (1913). See Bibliography.

[2] Reynolds and Goldsmith are notable omissions. Hughes says that "in his [Sir Joshua's] case the columns of Religion and Morality are left blank."

[3] *I.e.* "the Good Humour necessary to conversation."

is brought down by 3 for Scholarship and o for Good Humour; Seward's by o for Religion, Humour, and Good Humour; Boswell is bracketed top with Burney in Good Humour (19 marks), but only reaches half marks in two other subjects; Thrale begins well with 18 for Religion and 17 for Morality, but fails to score in Wit, Humour, or Good Humour; Burke's record is very similar to Thrale's; Baretti has a miserable score in everything except General Knowledge; James Harris has a low aggregate, but is the only member of the circle to be awarded full marks for Scholarship[1].

While Mrs Thrale need not be taken too seriously as an examiner, her assessments indicate a certain shrewdness. What is noticeable, in particular, is the severity of her marking for Wit and Humour. The only subject, on the other hand, in which a high average is maintained is General Knowledge; that, presumably, was the minimum demanded by an eighteenth-century *salonière*.

In any event Mrs Thrale must have enjoyed compiling this mark-sheet as much as she enjoyed writing the "little paltry verse characters" for the portraits which hung in the Streatham

[1] James Harris, known as 'Hermes' Harris, being the author of *Hermes, or a Philosophical Inquiry concerning Universal Grammar,* of which Mrs Thrale was given an interleaved copy. "Harris" said Johnson "is a sound sullen scholar; he does not like interlopers. Harris, however, is a prig, and a bad prig. I looked into his book and thought he did not understand his own system."

gallery. Her lines on Johnson are quoted in the *Anecdotes*[1].

A more important picture of the Streatham circle is that preserved in Fanny Burney's *Diary*. Very naturally, many of the conversations recorded in the period 1778–1784 are concerned with *Evelina* and its authorship, but no one has drawn a truer picture of the Johnson who, in the society of lively ladies, considered himself "a very polite man":

Dr Johnson (she wrote in August 1778) came home to dinner. In the evening he was as lively and full of wit and sport as I have ever seen him; and Mrs Thrale and I had him quite to ourselves; for Mr Thrale came in from giving an election dinner (to which he sent two bucks and six pine-apples) so tired, that he neither opened his eyes nor mouth, but fell fast asleep. Indeed, after tea he generally does. Dr Johnson was very communicative concerning his present work of the "Lives of the Poets"; Dryden is now in the press, and he told us he had been just writing a dissertation upon "Hudibras."

Johnson gave the ladies a Latin lesson every morning, but it was his merriment that impressed Fanny Burney:

Johnson has more fun, and comical humour, and love of nonsense about him, than almost anybody I ever saw: I mean when with those he likes; for otherwise, he can be as severe and as bitter as report relates him. Mrs Thrale has all that gaiety of disposition and lightness of heart, which commonly belong to fifteen.

[1] p. 189 of this edition; for the other 'verse characters' see Hayward, ii, 170.

To Johnson, indeed, the Thrale household was primarily not a *salon*, but a home. From the day that he was prevailed upon to quit his close habitation in Johnson's court[1] until the day of Henry Thrale's death, the house at Streatham was for him the firſt house in which he taſted the continuous joy of solid comfort. Of Johnson's pleasures (and no man, as he said, is a hypocrite in his pleasures) there was hardly one which he could not enjoy at Streatham—conversation, a good library, pretty women, late hours, careful cookery, fruit[2]. How different muſt the proof-correction of the *Lives of the Poets*, done in consultation with Fanny Burney in the summer-house (near the peach trees), have been from the final labours, performed "amidſt inconvenience and diſtraction, in sickness and in sorrow," upon the *Dictionary of the English Language*.

ℂ. *Johnson and Mrs Thrale* 1781–1784

When Thrale died, one thing was clear— Johnson could not have the same freedom of the house as before. Furthermore, the loss of Thrale in itself meant much to Johnson. Whatever Henry Thrale's failings may have been, he held a very definite and personal attraction for Johnson: "I am afraid of thinking of what I have loſt, I never had

---

[1] See p. 83.

[2] "We have not once missed a pine-apple since I came, and therefore you may imagine their abundance; besides grapes, melons, peaches, nectarines and ices."—Fanny Burney.

such a friend before" he wrote to Mrs Thrale on 9 April 1781; and again, two days later: "I feel myself like a man beginning a new course of life. I had interwoven myself with my dear friend."

The bitterest critic of Johnson cannot ascribe such feelings as these to mere cupboard-love. Apart from all the Streatham comforts, Johnson, for reasons which it is not wholly easy to discern, loved the man Henry Thrale for himself. Even if, after his death, his widow had given no particle of offence, Streatham could never have been the same to Johnson again[1]. Thrale's death closed an epoch.

For some time Johnson was busy as executor. He was dealing, in the words of Lord Lucan's famous story, quoted by Boswell, not with a parcel of boilers and vats, but with "the potentiality of growing rich beyond the dreams of avarice."

If an angel from heaven had told me twenty years ago (wrote Mrs Thrale) that the man I knew by the name of *Dictionary Johnson* should one day become partner with me in a great trade, and that we should jointly or separately sign notes, drafts &c. for three or four thousand pounds of a morning, how unlikely it would have seemed ever to happen....Johnson, however, who desires above all other good the accumulation of new ideas, is but too happy with his present employment....

Johnson was indeed the only one of the executors who was unwilling to sell the brewery, but Mrs

---

[1] "I passed the summer at Streatham, but there was no Thrale." Johnson to Langton, 20 March 1782.

Thrale was overjoyed when "God Almighty sent a knot of rich Quakers" who bought the whole business for £135,000. She had never been wholly free from resentment against her commercial connection, and so she wrote: "I will go to church, give God thanks, receive the Sacrament and forget the frauds, follies, and inconveniences of a commercial life."

For some time Johnson appears still to have regarded Streatham as his home. Early in June he made a little tour with Boswell to Squire Dilly's in Bedfordshire, but he spent the summer at Streatham[1], and when he set out on his journey to Oxford, Birmingham, Lichfield and Ashbourne in October, he declared that he hardly knew the motives of his journey.

In the early part of 1782 Johnson was "much out of order" and told Malone that for many weeks he had gone out only in a coach to Mrs Thrale's[2], where he could "use all the freedom that sickness requires."

In April he wrote, with obvious exaggeration, to Mrs Thrale: "I have been very much out of order since you sent me away; but why should I tell you, who do not care, nor desire to know?...."

At the beginning of June, however, he was suffi-

[1] On 9 August at 3 p.m. he retired to the summer-house "to plan a life of greater diligence." *Life*, IV, 135.
[2] "Such a place to visit nobody ever had."—Johnson to Mrs Thrale, 16 February 1782.

ciently recovered to dine on skate, pudding, goose, and Streatham asparagus; and shortly afterwards he prepared to go to Oxford. On 9 July Boswell wrote to Mrs Thrale in high spirits:

My dear Madam, from the day that I first had the pleasure to meet you, when I jumpt into your coach, not I hope from impudence, but from that agreable kind of attraction which makes one forget ceremony, I have invariably thought of you with admiration and gratitude. Were I to make out a chronological account of all the happy hours which I owe to you, I should appear under great debt, and debt of a peculiar nature, for a generous mind cannot be discharged of it by the creditor.

This is in the true Boswellian vein of gallantry and gusto. The purpose of the letter appears in the next paragraph:

May I presume still more upon your kindness, and beg that you may write to me at more length? I do not mean to put you to a great deal of trouble; but you write so easily that you might by a small expence of time give me much pleasure. Anecdotes of our literary or gay freinds, but particularly of our illustrious Imlac, would delight me[1].

Mrs Thrale was still an important authority for *Johnsoniana*. A phrase in Johnson's letter to Boswell of 24 August 1782 is also worthy of note: "If you desire to meet me at Ashbourne, I believe I can come thither; if you had rather come to London, I can stay at Streatham...."

---

[1] *Letters of James Boswell* (ed. Tinker), II, 313. This letter was first printed, though not quite accurately, in Broadley's *Doctor Johnson and Mrs Thrale*, p. 143.

This, as Hayward points out, was two days after Mrs Thrale had decided, according to the narrative in *Thraliana*, to give up the Streatham house. Johnson had thought well of the project and had wished her to put it into early execution. On 6 October he recited the famous prayer:

Almighty God, Father of all mercy, help me, by thy grace, that I may with humble and sincere thankfulness remember the comforts and conveniences which I have enjoyed at this place, and that I may resign them with holy submission....

There is sadness here, but, surely, no bitterness. Mrs Thrale, indeed, affected disappointment at Johnson's cool acceptance of the altered state of things. In a childish outburst she declared:

I begin to see...that Johnson's connection with me is merely an interested one; he *loved* Mr Thrale, I believe, but only wished to find in me a careful nurse and humble friend for his sick and his lounging hours....

However, instead of breaking away, Johnson accompanied Mrs Thrale to Brighton and stayed with her six weeks. Of this visit Fanny Burney gives a fairly full, and rather gloomy, account. Johnson was not, according to her, a *persona grata* amongst Mrs Thrale's Brighton friends. He went once to a ball, to avoid the greater evil of solitude, but was continually excepted from invitations, "either from too much respect or too much fear." Whether or no Mrs Thrale was herself responsible for the Doctor's black humour, Miss Burney makes it clear that Johnson was well-nigh unapproachable[1].

On his return to London, he recovered something of his sociability and Miss Burney found him "environed with listeners" at Miss Monckton's assembly on 8 December. About Christmas-time he was ill: "You can hardly think," he wrote to Mrs Thrale on 20 December, "how bad I have been while you were in all your altitudes, at the Opera, and all the fine places, and thinking little of me....I hope however to be with you in a short time...."

In March 1783 Boswell was "glad to find him at Mrs Thrale's house in Argyll St, appearances of friendship between them being still kept up." That there was still a little more than an 'appearance' of friendship is shown by Johnson's letters written to Bath, whither Mrs Thrale had gone in April:

Your last letter was very pleasing; it expressed kindness to me, and some degree of placid acquiescence in your present mode of life, which is, I think, the best which is at present within your reach (13 *June*).

Johnson, it is true, is querulous—he had a paralytic stroke about this time—and uneasy about the future. He hints that Mrs Thrale will pass over his letter of 19 June "with the careless glance of frigid indifference":

You see I yet turn to you with my complaints as a settled and unalienable friend; do not, do not drive me

[1] *Diary* (ed. 1891), I, 459.

from you, for I have not deserved either neglect or hatred...
I am almost ashamed of this querulous letter, but now it
is written, let it go.

Had Johnson the specific fear of the Piozzi
marriage in his mind when he wrote of being
driven away from his old friend? Certainly, he
had not been "called in to counsel on matters of
the heart[1]," and in June 1783 matters of the heart
occupied a large place in Mrs Thrale's life. Early
in the year she had, at the instance of her daughters
and of Miss Burney, sent Piozzi away; by June
she was sincerely regretting the sacrifice.

On hearing of Johnson's stroke, she offered to
come up from Bath. "Your offer, dear Madam, of
coming to me," wrote Johnson in reply, "is charm-
ingly kind; but I will lay it up for future use." In a
letter of 13 November his tone is still more tender:

Since you have written to me with the attention and
tenderness of ancient time, your letters give me a great
part of the pleasure which a life of solitude admits.

Miss Burney visited Johnson about a week later and
found him "more instructive, entertaining, good-
humoured, and exquisitely fertile, than ever[2]."

[1] Hayward, I, 197.
[2] *Diary*, I, 542. The often-quoted account, given in the
Memoirs of Dr Burney (II, 360 ff., ed. 1832), of the interview
at which Johnson, after hoarsely ejaculating: "Piozzi!" became
speechless with indignation, is obviously a much less trustworthy
authority than the *Diary*. No specific date is given to the interview in the *Memoirs*, but the context fixes it between 19 November and 30 December. It is hard to reconcile the story with
Johnson's letters belonging to this period.

The letters written by Johnson to Mrs Thrale in the spring of 1784 abound in medical details, but on 21 April he was able to send intelligence (which he hoped Mrs Thrale would not receive "without some degree of pleasure") that after a confinement of 129 days he had returned thanks to God in St Clement's Church for his recovery. His friends made haste to welcome him:

Now I am broken loose (he wrote on 13 May) my friends seem willing enough to see me. On Monday I dined with Paradise; Tuesday, Hoole; Wednesday, Dr Taylor; to-day, with Jodrel; Friday, Mrs Garrick; Saturday, Dr Brocklesby; next Monday, Dilly.

Meanwhile Mrs Thrale had sent for Piozzi[1], and a circular letter announcing her decision was sent to Johnson and the other guardians on 30 June.

To Johnson Mrs Thrale sent a covering letter in which she begged pardon for concealing the connexion with Piozzi.

Indeed, my dear Sir, (she wrote,) it was concealed only to save us both needless pain; I could not have borne to reject that counsel it would have killed me to take, and I only tell it you now because all is irrevocably settled, and out of your power to prevent. I will say, however, that the dread of your disapprobation has given me some anxious moments....

Johnson's reply was written in sorrowful anger:

If I interpret your letter right, you are ignominiously

[1] Her daughter Sophia is said to have realised in November 1783 that her mother's love for Piozzi was incurable and the daughters finally relented in May 1784 (Hayward, i, 219, 221).

married....If you have abandoned your children and your religion, God forgive your wickedness; if you have forfeited your fame and your country, may your folly do no further mischief....

This was written on 2 July. Two days later Mrs Piozzi wrote a spirited defence both of herself and of her second husband:

Never did I oppose your will, or control your wish; nor can your unmerited severity itself lessen my regard; but till you have changed your opinion of Mr Piozzi, let us converse no more. God bless you.

Evidently this letter made the right appeal both to Johnson's sense of justice and to his sense of gratitude. Common sense told him that it was no business of his to interfere and that, even if it were, the time for interference had gone by; his heart told him that, whatever happened, he could neither forget, nor repay, the happiness which the Thrales had given him. So, in his last letter, the bitterness of resentment gave place to "one sigh more of tenderness, perhaps useless, but at least sincere."

It has seemed worth while to trace this outline of the relations between Johnson and Mrs Thrale from the death of Thrale to the announcement of the Piozzi marriage, in order to do some measure of justice to both sides.

Macaulay's wild account of Mrs Thrale's "degrading passion" and of Johnson "leaving for ever that beloved home [Streatham] for the gloomy and desolate house behind Fleet Street, where the few and evil days which still remained to him were to

run out[1]" has long been discredited. That Mrs
Thrale wished to relax some of the ties which had
bound Johnson to her household is clear enough.
Thrale's death was, as she quickly realised, a
greater blow to Johnson than to herself. She could
still amuse and entertain Johnson, but she could
not (as her husband, in some mysterious way, had
done) command his respect. "There is," in Hayward's rather pompous phrasing, "a very great
difference, when arrangements are to be made for
the domestication of a male visitor, between a
family with a male head, and one consisting ex-
clusively of females."

Furthermore, though she could still discuss her
business or her children with Johnson, she did not
dare to broach the subject which really filled her
mind. It is a poor compliment to be trusted with
every confidence except the most important, and
the final revelation of *l'affaire Piozzi* was to
Johnson both a shock and a humiliation.

Probably Mrs Thrale knew her own business
best when she wrote to Johnson on 30 June 1784
that the concealment of her designs was due to a
desire to save needless pain on both sides; but it
is just conceivable that, had Johnson been made
sole confidant, he might have defended Piozzi
against the world.

Sir (we can hear him say to Boswell), never accustom
your mind to mingle headlong passion with sincere devotion. Here is a lady whose name has been shamelessly

---

[1] *Encyclopaedia Britannica* article on Samuel Johnson.

bandied about in the public prints by every scribbler accustomed to lie. To all such slanderers she has replied by conferring her affections upon an Italian gentleman of refined manners and elegant attainments. Sir, when you can earn as much by your pleading as Signor Piozzi by his playing, I shall be very ready to recommend you as a suitor.

The conjecture may seem fantastic, but did not Boswell, by masterly diplomacy, win Johnson to the side of John Wilkes?

From Johnson's point of view, Piozzi's nationality and profession[1] were both unfortunate; had he been an Englishman and, say, a schoolmaster, Johnson might have been his stoutest champion.

Perhaps the most comforting fact in the whole dreary controversy is that neither Johnson nor Mrs Piozzi ultimately bore malice. That Johnson meant what he wrote when, on first receiving the news of the marriage, he declaimed against Mrs Thrale's abandonment of her children and her religion need not be denied; but the truest note was struck when, less than a week later, he wrote:

I wish that God may grant you every blessing, that you may be happy in this world for its short continuance, and eternally happy in a better state; and whatever I can contribute to your happiness I am very ready to repay, for that kindness which soothed twenty years of a life radically wretched.

That, after all, was Johnson's final verdict upon Mrs Thrale, and it may suffice for us.

[1] "And pray, Sir, *who is Bach?* Is he a piper?"—Fanny Burney, *Early Diary*, ii, 156.

ℭ. *The Writings of Mrs Piozzi*

At an early age, Hester Salusbury had an itch
for writing:

> It was then, too, when I was about thirteen, fourteen,
> and fifteen years old, that I took a fancy to write in the
> "St James's Chronicle," unknown to my parents and my
> tutor too: it was my sport to see them reading, studying,
> blaming or praising their own little whimsical girl's per-
> formances....The little poetical trash I *did* write in *earnest*,
> is preserved somewhere, perhaps in "Thraliana," which I
> promised to Mrs Mostyn: perhaps in a small repository
> I prepared for dear Salusbury. There is a little poem
> called "Offley Park" I know; another "On my poor Aunt
> Anna Maria's favourite Ash Tree"; and one styled "The
> Old Hunter's Petition for Life," written to save dear
> Forester from being shot because grown superannuated...[1].

Mrs Thrale's verse was essentially of the 'Miscellany' order, and her poem entitled *The Three
Warnings* appeared in Mrs Anna Williams's *Miscellanies* of 1766. Even Boswell could not "with-
hold from Mrs Thrale the praise of being the
authour of that admirable poem."

Many other examples of Mrs Thrale's somewhat fanciful verses have been preserved. At
Florence in 1785 she collaborated with Robert
Merry ('Della Crusca' Merry), Bertie Greatheed
and William Parsons in producing *The Florence
Miscellany*, to which she contributed the Preface,
several poems, and the Conclusion.

[1] *Autobiographical Memoirs* (Hayward, II, 28).

In the Preface, which Horace Walpole described as "short and sensible and genteel," Mrs Piozzi is archly modest:

Our little Book can scarcely be less important to Readers of a distant Age or Nation than we ourselves are ready to acknowledge it...we shall at least be allow'd to have glisten'd innocently in Italian Sunshine, and to have imbibed from its rays the warmth of mutual Benevolence....

Mutual benevolence is indeed the keynote of the collection, and Gifford in his *Baviad* and *Mæviad* made fun of the whole 'Della Crusca' group.

See Thrale's grey widow with a satchel roam
And bring in pomp laborious nothings home.

It was from Florence that Mrs Piozzi wrote on 7 June 1785 to Mr Cadell, the bookseller in the Strand, offering the *Anecdotes* for publication. It appeared in the next year and had an immediate success. It was the first intimate study of Johnson, and four editions were printed within twelve months.

The *Anecdotes* are not great literature and do not pretend to be[1]. Horace Walpole was perhaps too severe in calling them "a heap of rubbish in a very vulgar style, and too void of method even for such a farrago"; but no one with a sense of literary form can wholly suppress a feeling of

---

[1] "The book is not faultless; but we should remember with the philosopher Ἔργμασιν ἐν μεγάλοις πᾶσιν ἀδεῖν χαλεπόν." From a MS note in an annotated copy of the *Anecdotes* in the British Museum.

irritation at the inconsequent way in which Mrs Piozzi handles her material. The anecdotes are brought together in a style which throws the magnificent orderliness of Boswell's narrative into high relief; and one feels towards Mrs Piozzi's writing something of what Johnson felt towards Poll Carmichael's conversation. Mrs Piozzi could never write "tightly and closely"; she was "wiggle waggle."

It would, however, be absurd to judge the *Anecdotes* by the unique biographical standard which was to be set by James Boswell. Mrs Piozzi herself was not blind to their limitations: "I must here take leave to observe," she writes, "that in giving little memoirs of Mr Johnson's behaviour and conversation, such as I saw and heard it, my book lies under manifest disadvantages...." It was the first book which Mrs Piozzi "ever presented before the Public" and it thoroughly justifies Sir Walter Raleigh's description of the author as a "lively, feather-headed lady." Witty in conversation and genuinely interested in literature, she had yet no sense of literary discipline.

Still, the *Anecdotes* have a real value, since Mrs Piozzi had had a unique opportunity of appraising Johnson in a domestic *milieu*. To her we owe many an 'exquisite trait' of Johnsonian character and conversation. The description of Bathurst as "a very good hater"; the reply to the complaint that beggars spend their halfpence on gin and tobacco: "And why should they be denied such sweeteners of existence?"; the retort to the 'disrespectful' young gentleman: "I would advise no man to marry, Sir, who is not likely to propagate understanding"—these and many others we owe to the 'little memoirs' of Mrs Piozzi.

As a book, the *Anecdotes* were not only a success, but a 'sensation.' The king sent for a copy on the evening of the day of publication, but there was no copy to be had. Cadell declared that he had never published such a rapid-selling book. The fourth edition appeared before the end of 1786.

Such a success was natural enough. Everyone was eager to read something new about Johnson[1], and, ever since the death of Henry Thrale, the journalists had made his widow a subject of perpetual gossip[2] and the Piozzi marriage set the seal upon her notoriety. When, therefore, "wafted by the gentle gales of Italy" the expected volume of *Anecdotes* arrived, the storm burst out afresh. Boswell's reply to the Postscript appeared in the *Gentleman's Magazine* for April 1786 and was in-

---

[1]   From beggars, to the GREAT who hold the helm,
      One *Johnso-mania* rag'd through all the realm.
                                        PETER PINDAR.

[2] "Lord Loughboro', Sir Richard Jebb, Mr Piozzi, Mr Selwyn, Dr Johnson, every man that comes to the house, is put in the papers for me to marry. In good time, I wrote to-day to beg the 'Morning Herald' would say no more about me, good or bad."—Hayward, I, 167.

corporated in the third edition of the *Tour*. Peter
Pindar's *Bozzy and Piozzi* quickly followed:

> At length, rush'd forth two CANDIDATES for fame;
> A SCOTCHMAN *one*, and one a LONDON DAME;
> *That*, by th' *emphatic* JOHNSON, christ'ned BOZZY;
> *This*, by the BISHOP'S license, DAME PIOZZI....

"Our comic performers" wrote Horace Walpole
"are Boswell and Dame Piozzi....The print-shops
teem with satiric prints on them." Some reviewers
were a little kinder, as one who wrote of the *Anecdotes* as an "agreeable parterre, which would have
been yet more fragrant if a few luxuriant shoots
had judiciously been pruned"; but right up to the
time of the publication of Boswell's *Life of Johnson*,
Mrs Piozzi was fair game for the versifiers. In
particular they resented her pretensions to learning:

> Mark! how the *ingenious Dame* of Streatham paid
> Her obsequies to *Doctor Johnson's* shade;
> *She*, wrapt in admiration, oft had hung
> O'er wondrous accents of his magic tongue;
> While, in her ear those fairy echoes play,
> And o'er her fond imagination stray,
> While such collective stores her memory fill,
> Ah, say! could *woman possibly be still!*...
> Ye fair, with kindlier charms by Nature grac'd
> For other studies cultivate a taste;
> Aim not, to wield the literary pen;
> Leave *Hebrew, Greek*, and *Latin* all to men[1].

But Mrs Piozzi, once launched on to the stormy
sea of authorship, showed no sign of laying down

---

[1] *Epistle to James Boswell*, 1790.

her pen. The *Letters to and from the late Samuel Johnson, LL.D.* were published in 1788 and raised another storm. The chief assailant was Baretti who wrote a series of three 'Strictures' in the *European Magazine*. Baretti had his own quarrel with 'La Piozzi' and his invective is brutal and wearisome. At the end of the second 'Stricture' comes this paragraph:

> Who knows, I say, but some one of our modern dramatick geniuses may hereafter entertain the public with a laughable comedy in five long acts, intitled with singular propriety The SCIENTIFIC MOTHER?

From this the inference seems fairly clear that *The Sentimental Mother, A comedy in five acts; The Legacy of an Old Friend, and his Last Moral Lesson to Mrs Hester Lynch Thrale, now Mrs Hetser* [sic] *Lynch Piozzi* (1789) is the work of Joseph Baretti.

If the play created any impression at all, it would seem more likely to have roused sympathy for, rather than against, Mrs Piozzi. For whatever that lady's weaknesses may have been, she never approached the vulgar fatuity of Lady Fantasma Tunskull in *The Sentimental Mother*. Here is one of Lady Fantasma's less offensive speeches:

> What was I saying, Sir. Oh—I have really made a human creature of Mr Prettyman. He could neither eat, drink, or speak like a Christian, till I took pains with him. And the effect is wonderful. The whole neighbourhood of Brazenhall rings with my praises and says it is a pity forsooth I am a woman. I ought to have been at the head

of a college; (*a little pause in which she is disappointed, that Mr Bellamy does not echo her praises*)—You won't go with me, Captain Bellamy, I suppose—You had rather be with the girls: you are very sly and mischievous.

More important are Baretti's *marginalia* on a copy of the *Letters* preserved in the British Museum. The student will find them duly incorporated in the notes to Birkbeck Hill's edition. While Mrs Piozzi deliberately omitted names and paragraphs from Johnson's letters, it is unlikely that she was guilty of 'clumsy fabrications'[1]. Did Johnson refer to the tyranny of Baretti over Mrs Thrale's children?[2] Did he write of Boswell: "One would think the man had been hired to be a spy upon me"?[3] Birkbeck Hill thinks it "very improbable" that Johnson wrote this latter sentence. But why? Johnson could be very rude to Boswell the note-taker and the remark accords well enough with the famous incident described in the *Memoirs of Dr Burney*: "What do you do there, sir?—Go to the table, sir!" Certainly Mrs Piozzi did not publish the complete correspondence relating to her second marriage, but Baretti's accusation that Johnson's final letter was a forgery is wholly unfounded.

Controversy apart, the *Letters* are valuable evidence both of Johnson's epistolary style and of the

[1] See Mr R. W. Chapman's letter in the *Times Literary Supplement* of 30 Oct. 1924.
[2] Letter 420 (Hill's edition). [3] Letter 405 (Hill's edition).

relations between him and the Streatham household. They show Johnson's capacity for playful-
ness and his very human love of gossip:

Such tattle as filled your laſt sweet letter prevents one
great inconvenience of absence, that of returning home a
ſtranger and an enquirer. The variations of life consiſt
of little things. Important innovations are soon heard and
easily underſtood. Men that meet to talk of physics or
metaphysics, or law or hiſtory, may be immediately acquainted. We look at each other in silence, only for want
of petty talk upon slight occurrences. Continue to write
all that you would say.

Still more ſtriking is Johnson's gratification at
being accepted as a real family friend:

I cannot but think on your kindness and my maſter's.
Life has, upon the whole, fallen short, very short, of my
early expeċtation; but the acquisition of such a friendship,
at an age when new friendships are seldom acquired, is
something better than the general course of things gives
man a right to expect. I think on it with great delight,
I am not very apt to be delighted.

Reference has already been made to the serious-
ness with which Johnson assumed a share in the
responsibilities in the brewing business. He
watched the harvest with a keen eye to the barley
prospects, and ordered Frank "to make his observations" as they drove to Lichfield.

The harveſt is abundant (he wrote), and the weather
à la merveille. No season ever was finer. Barley, malt,
beer, and money.

In 1789 Mrs Piozzi published her *Observations and Refleċtions made in the course of a journey*

through France, Italy, and Germany, in two volumes. It is a work highly characteristic of the "lively, feather-headed lady's" pen; a work into which it is agreeable to dip and find a story like the following:

Mr Udney the British Consul [at Leghorn, whence the *Anecdotes* "took their flight for England"] is alone now...we saw his fine collection of pictures, among which is a Danae that once belonged to Queen Christina of Sweden, and fell from her possession into that of some nobleman, who being tormented by scruples of morality upon his death-bed, resolved to part with all his undraped figures, but not liking to lose the face of this Danae, put the picture into a painter's hands to cut and clothe her; the man, instead of obeying orders he considered as barbarous, copied the whole and dressed the copy decently, sending it to his sick friend, who never discerned the trick; and kept the original to dispose of, where fewer scruples impeded an advantageous sale.

But if we are asked to "wade through two octavos," as Horace Walpole rather brutally put it, "of Dame Piozzi's *though*'s and *so*'s and *I trow*'s"[1] we may perhaps be permitted to retort: "Sir, do *you* read books through?"

Much the same might be said of *British Synonymy; or, an attempt at regulating the choice of words in familiar conversation* (1794). In her *Preface,* Mrs Piozzi declares herself to be persuaded that "while men teach to write with propriety, a woman may at worst be qualified—through

[1] See, for example, the sentence at the top of page 121 of the first volume.

long practice—to direct the choice of phrases in familiar talk." The work, which is in two volumes, contains a series of short expositions of the differences in meaning between groups of synonyms: *Gay, Lively, Pleasant, Facetious, Cheerful, Blythe,* or *Pious, Religious, Devout,* or *Main, Ocean, Sea,* or *Primate, Archbishop, Metropolitan.* These expositions are full of antiquarian and literary gossip and Johnson is often quoted; thus in the section dealing with the meanings of *Silly, Ignorant, Senseless* we read:

Doctor Johnson's story of a young woman he once knew, who laid by the bones off her own plate at dinner, when she had been eating chicken, to feed a friend's horse whom she expected to call in the evening, used to furnish us matter of dispute. I thought her an *idiot,* while he contended that she was only IGNORANT of what a milliner's prentice had no means of knowing. She did not betray symptoms of folly in her business, said he, nor yet dream of laying up oats and hay to feed the lap-dog—however she might mistake the nature of an animal who came little in her way, and might be carnivorous for aught she had opportunity to observe.

The syntax is not faultless, but the anecdote has the true ring of Johnson talking for victory, even in trifles.

But the most ambitious of all Mrs Piozzi's literary projects was *Retrospection: or A Review of the most striking and important events, characters, situations, and their consequences, which the last eighteen hundred years have presented to the view of mankind* (1801).

Mrs Piozzi's motives anticipated, in some measure, those of Mr H. G. Wells:

To our disturbed and busy days abridgments only can be useful. No one has leisure to read better books. Young people are called out to act before they *know*, before they could have *learned* how those have acted who have lived before them.

Retrospection is not a critical history:

History herself is often ill prepared enough when sudden questions interrupt her eloquence; and my poor summary is willing to confess as controvertible the truth of many a fact recorded here: but with the facts, except as a compiler, myself have nought to do[1].

These are the true accents of "your poor little H. L. P."; but one cannot but admire the courage that impelled a lady of nearly sixty years of age to begin with "Chapter I, Containing the First Century from Tiberius to Trajan" and to fill nearly one thousand quarto pages, the last of them dealing with the years 1796–1800.

Only one more work of Mrs Piozzi remains to be briefly mentioned: *Love Letters of Mrs Piozzi, written when she was eighty, to William Augustus Conway* (1843).

Conway was an actor who appeared first at Covent Garden in 1813 and subsequently played many parts in Shakespearean tragedy. He was

[1] Vol. I, p. 185.

extremely good-looking, but not an actor of the first rank. In America he was no more successful than in England and, on a voyage from New York to Charleston in 1828, he jumped overboard and was drowned. Among his possessions brought back from New York was a packet of letters from his "dearly attached friend, the celebrated Mrs Piozzi." The letters were lent to a gentleman who copied them and had them printed in 1843.

Such is the story given in the *Preface* to the *Love Letters*. These letters have provoked a mild controversy. Mrs Piozzi's champions[1] throw doubt upon their authenticity; on the other hand it was stated in the *New Monthly Magazine* for April 1861 that Charles Mathews had seen a letter from Mrs Piozzi, offering to marry Conway.

What does it matter? Internal evidence suggests that the *Love Letters* are genuine enough. But how can we discover or define the motives of a sentimental and vivacious old lady writing to a handsome young actor? Is an exact meaning to be attributed even to a passage like this?

This is Preaching...but remember how the Sermon is written at three, four, and five o'clock by an Octogenary pen...a Heart (as Mrs Lee says) 26 years old: and as H. L. P. feels it to be;—ALL YOUR OWN.

---

[1] Hayward, *Autobiography of Mrs Piozzi*, I, 359. Seeley, *Mrs Thrale*, 328. Seccombe, Introductory Essay in Broadley, *Doctor Johnson and Mrs Thrale*, 60, 61. See also Knapp, *Piozzi-Pennington Letters*, 305, 306.

We may do well to recall Johnson's reply to the nameless clergyman at Streatham:

> Were not Dodd's sermons addressed to the passions?
> JOHNSON. They were nothing, Sir, be they addressed to what they may.

In a Family Bible, printed at Stourbridge in 1811 and preserved in the British Museum, there is an inscription on the fly-leaf stating that the book was the property of Mrs Susanna Rudd[1], of Clifton, and was intrusted to the care of H. L. P., who "restored the Text and wrote Notes to it."

These notes are further evidence of the volubility of the "Octogenary pen." The following are characteristic specimens:

On *Genesis* xxviii

There *was* a black stone at Strawberry Hill in Mr Walpole's Time which I have heard Lysons and Lloyd of Wygfair say…possessed some extraordinary qualities… but everybody is dead now 1820 except poor H. L. P.

on *Genesis* xl. 23

I dare say he did.

on *Leviticus* xxiii. 24

We call it All Souls Day and in N. Wales it is observed by lighting fires on the Hills to this hour; Archbp Usher and the great Chronologer Mr Bedford think this was the day on which Adam fell.

---

[1] Frequently mentioned in the *Piozzi-Pennington Letters*.

on *Revelation* xiii. 11

Perhaps Buonaparte who pretended gentleness at the first but soon spake as a dragon.

At the beginning there are some characteristic verses in honour of the Progress of Science and scraps of Greek and Hebrew are scattered throughout the margins of the book.

So, to the end (and in an admirable handwriting) Mrs Piozzi preserved her activity both of tongue and pen.

ANECDOTES

OF THE LATE

SAMUEL JOHNSON, LL.D.

DURING THE LAST

TWENTY YEARS OF HIS LIFE.

BY

HESTHER LYNCH PIOZZI.

THE FOURTH EDITION.

LONDON:

PRINTED FOR T. CADELL IN THE STRAND.

MDCCLXXXVI.

PREFACE.

I HAVE somewhere heard or read, that the Preface before a book, like the portico before a house, should be contrived, so as to catch, but not detain the attention of those who desire admission to the family within, or leave to look over the collection of pictures made by one whose opportunities of obtaining them we know to have been not unfrequent. I wish not to keep my readers long from such intimacy with the manners of Dr. Johnson, or such knowledge of his sentiments as these pages can convey. To urge my distance from England as an excuse for the book's being ill written, would be ridiculous; it might indeed serve as a just reason for my having written it at all; because, though others may print the same aphorisms and stories, I cannot *here* be sure that they have done so. As the Duke says however to the Weaver, in A Midsummer Night's Dream, "Never excuse; if your play be a bad one, keep at least the excuses to yourself."

I am aware that many will say, I have not spoken highly enough of Dr. Johnson; but it will be difficult for those who say so, to speak more highly. If I have described his manners as they were, I have been careful to shew his superiority to the common forms of common life. It is surely no dispraise to an oak that it does not bear jessamine; and he who should plant honeysuckle round Trajan's column, would not be thought to adorn, but to disgrace it.

When I have said, that he was more a man of genius than of learning, I mean not to take from the one part of his character that which I willingly give to the other. The erudition of Mr. Johnson proved his genius; for he had not acquired it by long or profound study: nor can I think those characters the greatest which have most learning driven into their heads, any more than I can persuade myself to consider the river Jenisca as superior to the Nile, because the first receives near seventy tributary streams in the course of its unmarked progress to the sea, while the great parent of African plenty, flowing from an almost invisible source, and unenriched by any extraneous waters, except eleven nameless rivers, pours his majestic torrents into the ocean by seven celebrated mouths.

But I must conclude my Preface, and begin my book, the first I ever presented before the Public; from whose awful appearance in some measure to defend and conceal myself, I have thought fit to retire behind the Telamonian shield, and shew as little of myself as possible; well aware of the exceeding difference there is, between fencing in the school and fighting in the field.——Studious however to avoid offending, and careless of that offence which can be taken without a cause, I here not unwillingly submit my slight performance to the decision of that glorious country, which I have the daily delight to hear applauded in others, as eminently just, generous, and humane.

ANECDOTES *of the* LATE
SAMUEL JOHNSON, *LL.D.*

TOO much intelligence is often as pernicious to Biography as too little; the mind remains perplexed by contradiction of probabilities, and finds difficulty in separating report from truth. If Johnson then lamented that so little had ever been said about Butler, I might with more reason be led to complain that so much has been said about himself; for numberless informers but distract or cloud information, as glasses which multiply will for the most part be found also to obscure. Of a life, too, which for the last twenty years was passed in the very front of literature, every leader of a literary company, whether officer or subaltern, naturally becomes either author or critic, so that little less than the recollection that it was *once* the request of the deceased, and *twice* the desire of those whose will I ever delighted to comply with, should have engaged me to add my little book to the number of those already written on the subject. I used to urge another reason for forbearance, and say, that all the readers would, on this singular occasion, be the writers of his life: like the first representation of the Masque of Comus, which, by changing their characters from spectators to performers, was *acted* by the lords and ladies it was *written* to entertain. This objection is however now at an end, as I have found friends, far remote indeed from literary questions, who may yet be diverted from melancholy by my description of Johnson's manners, warmed to virtue even by the distant reflexion of his glowing excellence, and encouraged by the relation of his animated zeal to persist in the profession as well as practice of Christianity.

SAMUEL JOHNSON was the son of Michael Johnson, a bookseller at Litchfield, in Staffordshire; a very pious and worthy man, but wrongheaded, positive, and afflicted with melancholy, as his son, from whom alone I had the information, once told me: his business, however, leading him to be much on horseback, contributed to the preservation of his bodily health, and mental sanity; which, when he staid long at home, would sometimes be about to give way; and Mr. Johnson said, that when his work-shop, a detached building, had fallen half down for want of money to repair it, his father was not less diligent to lock the door every night, though he saw that any body might walk in at the back part, and knew that there was no security obtained by barring the front door. "*This* (says his son) was madness, you may see, and would have been discoverable in other instances of the prevalence of imagination, but that poverty prevented it from playing such tricks as riches and leisure encourage." Michael was a man of still larger size and greater strength than his son, who was reckoned very like him, but did not delight in talking much of his family—"one has (says he) *so* little pleasure in reciting the anecdotes of beggary." One day, however, hearing me praise a favourite friend with partial tenderness as well as true esteem; "Why do you like that man's acquaintance so?" said he: Because, replied I, he is open and confiding, and tells me stories of his uncles and cousins; I love the light parts of a solid character. "Nay, if you are for family history (says Mr. Johnson good-humouredly), *I* can fit you: I had an uncle, Cornelius Ford, who, upon a journey, stopped and read an inscription written on a stone he saw standing by the way-side, set up, as it proved, in honour of a man who had leaped a certain leap thereabouts, the extent of which was specified upon the stone: Why now, says my uncle, I could leap it in my boots; and he did leap it in his boots. I had likewise another uncle, Andrew, continued he, my father's brother, who kept the ring in Smithfield (where they wrestled and boxed) for a whole year, and never was thrown or conquered. Here now are uncles for you, Mistress, if that's the way to your heart." Mr. Johnson was very conversant in the art of attack and defence by boxing, which science he had learned from this uncle Andrew, I believe; and I have heard him descant upon the age when people were received, and when rejected, in the schools once held for that brutal amusement, much to the admiration of those who had no expectation of his skill in such matters, from the sight of a figure which precluded all possibility of personal prowess; though, because he saw Mr. Thrale one day leap over a cabriolet stool, to shew that he was not tired after a chace of fifty miles or more, *he* suddenly jumped over it too; but in a way so strange and so unwieldy, that our terror lest he should break his bones, took from us even the power of laughing.

Michael Johnson was past fifty years old when he married his wife, who was upwards of forty; yet I think her son told me she remained three years childless before he was born into the world, who so greatly contributed to improve it. In three years more she brought another son, Nathaniel, who lived to be twenty-seven or twenty-eight years old, and of whose manly spirit I have heard his brother speak with pride and pleasure, mentioning one circumstance, particular enough, that when the company were one day lamenting the badness of the roads, he enquired where they could be, as he travelled the country more than most people, and had never seen a bad road in his life. The two brothers did not, however, much delight in each other's company, being always rivals for the mother's fondness; and many of the severe reflections on domestic life in Rasselas, took their source from its author's keen recollections of the time passed in his early years. Their father Michael died of an inflammatory fever, at the age of seventy-six, as Mr. Johnson told me: their mother at eighty-nine, of a gradual decay. She was slight in her person, he said, and rather below than above the common size. So excellent was her character, and so blameless her life, that when an oppressive neighbour once endeavoured to take from her a little field she possessed, he could persuade no attorney to undertake the cause against a woman so beloved in her narrow circle: and it is this incident he alludes to in the line of his Vanity of Human Wishes, calling her

The general favourite as the general friend.

Nor could any one pay more willing homage to such a character, though she had not been related to him, than did Dr. Johnson on every occasion that offered: his disquisition on Pope's epitaph placed over Mrs. Corbet, is a proof of that preference always given by him to a noiseless life over a bustling one; for however taste begins, we almost always see that it ends in simplicity; the glutton finishes by losing his relish for any thing highly sauced, and calls for his boiled chicken at the close of many years spent in the search of dainties; the connoisseurs are soon weary of Rubens, and the critics of Lucan; and the refinements of every kind heaped upon civil life, always sicken their possessors before the close of it.

At the age of two years Mr. Johnson was brought up to London by his mother, to be touched by Queen Anne for the scrophulous evil, which terribly afflicted his childhood, and left such marks as greatly disfigured a countenance naturally harsh and rugged, beside doing irreparable damage to the auricular organs, which never could perform their functions since I knew him; and it was owing to that horrible disorder, too, that one eye was perfectly useless to him; that defect, however, was not observable, the eyes looked both alike. As Mr. Johnson had an astonishing memory, I asked him, if he could remember Queen Anne at all? "He had (he said) a confused, but somehow a sort of solemn recollection of a lady in diamonds, and a long black hood."

The christening of his brother he remembered with all its circumstances, and said, his mother taught him to spell and pronounce the words *little Natty*, syllable by syllable, making him say it over in the evening to her husband and his guests. The trick which most parents play with their children, of shewing off their newly-acquired accomplishments, disgusted Mr. Johnson beyond expression; he had been treated so himself, he said, till he absolutely loathed his father's caresses, because he knew they were sure to precede some unpleasing display of his early abilities; and he used, when neighbours came o'visiting, to run up a tree that he might not be found and exhibited, such, as no doubt he was, a prodigy of early understanding. His epitaph upon the duck he killed by treading on it at five years old,

> Here lies poor duck
>   That Samuel Johnson trod on;
> If it had liv'd it had been good luck,
>   For it would have been an odd one;

is a striking example of early expansion of mind, and knowledge of language; yet he always seemed more mortified at the recollection of the bustle his parents made with his wit, than pleased with the thoughts of possessing it. "That (said he to me one day) is the great misery of late marriages; the unhappy produce of them becomes the plaything of dotage: an old man's child (continued he) leads much such a life, I think, as a little boy's dog, teized with awkward fondness, and forced, perhaps, to sit up and beg, as we call it, to divert a company, who at last go away complaining of their disagreeable entertainment." In consequence of these maxims, and full of indignation against such parents as delight to produce their young ones early into the talking world, I have known Mr. Johnson give a good deal of pain, by refusing to hear the verses the children could recite, or the songs they could sing; particularly one friend who told him that his two sons should repeat Gray's Elegy to him alternately, that he might judge who had the happiest cadence. "No, pray Sir (said he), let the dears both speak it at once; more noise will by that means be made, and the noise will be sooner over." He told me the story himself, but I have forgot who the father was.

Mr. Johnson's mother was daughter to a gentleman in the country, such as there were many of in those days, who possessing, perhaps, one or two hundred pounds a year in land, lived on the profits, and sought not to increase their income: she was

therefore inclined to think higher of herself than
of her husband, whose conduct in money matters
being but indifferent, she had a trick of teizing him
about it, and was, by her son's account, very im-
portunate with regard to her fears of spending
more than they could afford, though she never
arrived at knowing how much that was; a fault
common, as he said, to most women who pride
themselves on their œconomy. They did not however, as I could understand, live ill together on the
whole: "my father (says he) could always take his
horse and ride away for orders when things went
badly." The lady's maiden name was Ford; and
the parson who sits next to the punch-bowl in
Hogarth's Modern Midnight Conversation was
her brother's son. This Ford was a man who chose
to be eminent only for vice, with talents that might
have made him conspicuous in literature, and respectable in any profession he could have chosen:
his cousin has mentioned him in the lives of Fenton
and of Broome; and when he spoke of him to me,
it was always with tenderness, praising his acquaintance with life and manners, and recollecting one
piece of advice that no man surely ever followed
more exactly: "Obtain (says Ford) some general
principles of every science; he who can talk only
on one subject, or act only in one department, is
seldom wanted, and perhaps never wished for;
while the man of general knowledge can often
benefit, and always please." He used to relate,

however, another story less to the credit of his
cousin's penetration, how Ford on some occasion
said to him, "You will make your way the more
easily in the world, I see, as you are contented to
dispute no man's claim to conversation excellence;
they will, therefore, more willingly allow your pretensions as a writer." Can one, on such an occasion,
forbear recollecting the predictions of Boileau's
father, when stroaking the head of the young
satirist, *Ce petit bon homme* (says he) *n'à point trop
d'esprit*, mais il ne *dira jamais mal de personne*. Such
are the prognostics formed by men of wit and sense,
as these two certainly were, concerning the future
character and conduct of those for whose welfare
they were honestly and deeply concerned; and so
late do those features of peculiarity come to their
growth, which mark a character to all succeeding
generations.

Dr. Johnson first learned to read of his mother
and her old maid Catharine, in whose lap he well
remembered sitting while she explained to him the
story of St. George and the Dragon. I know not
whether this is the proper place to add, that such
was his tenderness, and such his gratitude, that he
took a journey to Litchfield fifty-seven years afterwards to support and comfort her in her last illness;
he had enquired for his nurse, and she was dead.
The recollection of such reading as had delighted
him in his infancy, made him always persist in
fancying that it was the only reading which could

please an infant; and he used to condemn me for putting Newbery's books into their hands as too trifling to engage their attention. "Babies do not want (said he) to hear about babies; they like to be told of giants and castles, and of somewhat which can stretch and stimulate their little minds." When in answer I would urge the numerous editions and quick sale of Tommy Prudent or Goody Two Shoes: "Remember always (said he) that the parents *buy* the books, and that the children never read them." Mrs. Barbauld however had his best praise, and deserved it; no man was more struck than Mr. Johnson with voluntary descent from possible splendour to painful duty.

At eight years old he went to school, for his health would not permit him to be sent sooner; and at the age of ten years his mind was disturbed by scruples of infidelity, which preyed upon his spirits, and made him very uneasy; the more so, as he revealed his uneasiness to no one, being naturally (as he said) "of a sullen temper and reserved disposition." He searched, however, diligently but fruitlessly, for evidences of the truth of revelation; and at length recollecting a book he had once seen in his father's shop, intitled, *De Veritate Religionis*, *&c.* he began to think himself highly culpable for neglecting such a means of information, and took himself severely to task for this sin, adding many acts of voluntary, and to others unknown, penance. The first opportunity which offered (of course) he seized the book with avidity; but on examination, not finding himself scholar enough to peruse its contents, set his heart at rest; and, not thinking to enquire whether there were any English books written on the subject, followed his usual amusements, and considered his conscience as lightened of a crime. He redoubled his diligence to learn the language that contained the information he most wished for; but from the pain which guilt had given him, he now began to deduce the soul's immortality, which was the point that belief first stopped at; and from that moment resolving to be a Christian, became one of the most zealous and pious ones our nation ever produced. When he had told me this odd anecdote of his childhood; "I cannot imagine (said he) what makes me talk of myself to you so, for I really never mentioned this foolish story to any body except Dr. Taylor, not even to my *dear dear* Bathurst, whom I loved better than ever I loved any human creature; but poor Bathurst is dead!!!"—Here a long pause and a few tears ensued. Why Sir, said I, how like is all this to Jean Jaques Rousseau! as like, I mean, as the sensations of frost and fire, when my child complained yesterday that the ice she was eating *burned* her mouth. Mr. Johnson laughed at the incongruous ideas; but the first thing which presented itself to the mind of an ingenious and learned friend whom I had the pleasure to pass some time with here at Florence, was the same resemblance, though I

think the two characters had little in common,
further than an early attention to things beyond
the capacity of other babies, a keen sensibility of
right and wrong, and a warmth of imagination
little consistent with sound and perfect health. I
have heard him relate another odd thing of himself
too, but it is one which every body has heard as
well as I: how, when he was about nine years old,
having got the play of Hamlet in his hand, and
reading it quietly in his father's kitchen, he kept
on steadily enough, till coming to the Ghost scene,
he suddenly hurried up stairs to the street door that
he might see people about him: such an incident,
as he was not unwilling to relate it, is probably in
every one's possession now; he told it as a testimony
to the merits of Shakespeare: but one day when
my son was going to school, and dear Dr. Johnson
followed as far as the garden gate, praying for his
salvation, in a voice which those who listened
attentively could hear plain enough, he said to me
suddenly, "Make your boy tell you his dreams:
the first corruption that entered into my heart was
communicated in a dream." What was it, Sir?
said I. "*Do* not ask me," replied he with much
violence, and walked away in apparent agitation.
I never durst make any further enquiries. He
retained a strong aversion for the memory of
Hunter, one of his schoolmasters, who, he said
once, was a brutal fellow: "so brutal (added he),
that no man who had been educated by him ever

sent his son to the same school." I have however heard him acknowledge his scholarship to be very great. His next master he despised, as knowing less than himself, I found; but the name of that gentleman has slipped my memory. Mr. Johnson was himself exceedingly disposed to the general indulgence of children, and was even scrupulously and ceremoniously attentive not to offend them: he had strongly persuaded himself of the difficulty people always find to erase early impressions either of kindness or resentment, and said, "he should never have so loved his mother when a man, had she not given him coffee she could ill afford, to gratify his appetite when a boy." If you had had children Sir, said I, would you have taught them any thing? "I hope (replied he), that I should have willingly lived on bread and water to obtain instruction for them; but I would not have set their future friendship to hazard for the sake of thrusting into their heads knowledge of things for which they might not perhaps have either taste or necessity. You teach your daughters the diameters of the planets, and wonder when you have done that they do not delight in your company. No science can be communicated by mortal creatures without attention from the scholar; no attention can be obtained from children without the infliction of pain, and pain is never remembered without resentment." That something should be learned, was however so certainly his opinion, that

I have heard him say, how education had been often compared to agriculture, yet that it resembled it chiefly in this: "that if nothing is sown, no crop (says he) can be obtained." His contempt of the lady who fancied her son could be eminent without study, because Shakespeare was found wanting in scholastic learning, was expressed in terms so gross and so well known, I will not repeat them here.

To recollect, however, and to repeat the sayings of Dr. Johnson, is almost all that can be done by the writers of his life; as his life, at least since my acquaintance with him, consisted in little else than talking, when he was not absolutely employed in some serious piece of work; and whatever work he did, seemed so much below his powers of performance, that he appeared the idlest of all human beings; ever musing till he was called out to converse, and conversing till the fatigue of his friends, or the promptitude of his own temper to take offence, consigned him back again to silent meditation.

The remembrance of what had passed in his own childhood, made Mr. Johnson very solicitous to preserve the felicity of children; and when he had persuaded Dr. Sumner to remit the tasks usually given to fill up boys' time during the holidays, he rejoiced exceedingly in the success of his negociation, and told me that he had never ceased representing to all the eminent schoolmasters in England, the absurd tyranny of poisoning the hour of permitted pleasure, by keeping future misery before the children's eyes, and tempting them by bribery or falsehood to evade it. "Bob Sumner (said he), however, I have at length prevailed upon: I know not indeed whether his tenderness was persuaded, or his reason convinced, but the effect will always be the same." Poor Dr. Sumner died, however, before the next vacation.

Mr. Johnson was of opinion, too, that young people should have *positive* not *general* rules given for their direction. "My mother (said he) was always telling me that I did not *behave* myself properly; that I should endeavour to learn *behaviour*, and such cant: but when I replied, that she ought to tell me what to do, and what to avoid, her admonitions were commonly, for that time at least, at an end."

This, I fear, was however at best a momentary refuge, found out by perverseness. No man knew better than Johnson in how many nameless and numberless actions *behaviour* consists: actions which can scarcely be reduced to rule, and which come under no description. Of these he retained so many very strange ones, that I suppose no one who saw his odd manner of gesticulating, much blamed or wondered at the good lady's solicitude concerning her son's *behaviour*.

Though he was attentive to the peace of children in general, no man had a stronger contempt than he for such parents as openly profess that they cannot govern their children. "How (says he) is an army governed? Such people, for the most part, multiply prohibitions till obedience becomes impossible, and authority appears absurd; and never suspect that they tease their family, their friends, and themselves, only because conversation runs low, and something must be said."

Of parental authority, indeed, few people thought with a lower degree of estimation. I one day mentioned the resignation of Cyrus to his father's will, as related by Xenophon, when, after all his conquests, he requested the consent of Cambyses to his marriage with a neighbouring princess; and I added Rollin's applause and recommendation of the example. "Do you not perceive then (says Johnson), that Xenophon on this occasion commends like a pedant, and Pere Rollin applauds like a slave? If Cyrus by his conquests had not purchased emancipation, he had conquered to little purpose indeed. Can you bear to see the folly of a fellow who has in his care the lives of thousands, when he begs his papa permission to be married, and confesses his inability to decide in a matter which concerns no man's happiness but his own?"—Mr. Johnson caught me another time reprimanding the daughter of my housekeeper for having sat down unpermitted in her mother's presence. "Why, she gets her living, does she not (said he), without her mother's help? Let the wench alone," continued he. And when we were again out of the women's sight who were concerned in the dispute: "Poor people's children, dear Lady (said he), never respect them: I did not respect my own mother, though I loved her: and one day, when in anger she called me a puppy, I asked her if she knew what they called a puppy's mother." We were talking of a young fellow who used to come often to the house; he was about fifteen years old, or less, if I remember right, and had a manner at once sullen and sheepish. "That lad (says Mr. Johnson) looks like the son of a schoolmaster; which (added he) is one of the very worst conditions of childhood: such a boy has no father, or worse than none; he never can reflect on his parent but the reflection brings to his mind some idea of pain inflicted, or of sorrow suffered."

I will relate one thing more that Dr. Johnson said about babyhood before I quit the subject; it was this: "That little people should be encouraged always to tell whatever they hear particularly striking, to some brother, sister, or servant, immediately before the impression is erased by the intervention of newer occurrences. He perfectly remembered the first time he ever heard of Heaven and Hell (he said), because when his mother had made out such a description of both places as she thought likely to seize the attention of her infant auditor, who was then in bed with her, she got up, and dressing him before the usual time, sent him directly to call a favourite workman in the house, to whom she knew he would communicate the conversation while it was yet impressed upon his mind. The event was what she wished, and it was to that method chiefly that he owed his uncommon felicity of remembering distant occurrences, and long past conversations."

At the age of eighteen Dr. Johnson quitted school, and escaped from the tuition of those he hated or those he despised. I have heard him relate very few college adventures. He used to say that our best accounts of his behaviour there would be gathered from Dr. Adams and Dr. Taylor, and that he was sure they would always tell the truth. He told me however one day, how, when he was first entered at the university, he passed a morning, in compliance with the customs of the place, at his tutor's chambers; but finding him no scholar, went no more. In about ten days after, meeting the same gentleman, Mr. Jordan, in the street, he offered to pass by without saluting him; but the tutor stopped, and enquired, not roughly neither, What he had been doing? "Sliding on the ice," was the reply; and so turned away with disdain. He laughed very heartily at the recollection of his own insolence, and said they endured it from him with wonderful acquiescence, and a gentleness that, whenever he thought of it, astonished himself. He told me too, that when he made his first declamation, he wrote over but one copy, and that coarsely; and having given it into the hand of the tutor who

ſtood to receive it as he passed, was obliged to
begin by chance and continue on how he could,
for he had got but little of it by heart; so fairly
truſting to his present powers for immediate
supply, he finished by adding aſtonishment to the
applause of all who knew how little was owing to
ſtudy. A prodigious risque, however, said some
one: "Not at all (exclaims Johnson), no man I
suppose leaps at once into deep water who does
not know how to swim."

I doubt not but this ſtory will be told by many
of his biographers, and said so to him when he told
it me on the 18th of July 1773. "And who will
be my biographer (said he), do you think?" Goldsmith, no doubt, replied I, and he will do it the
beſt among us. "The dog would write it beſt to be
sure, replied he; but his particular malice towards
me, and general disregard for truth, would make
the book useless to all, and injurious to my cha-
raĉter." Oh! as to that, said I, we should all faſten
upon him, and force him to do you juſtice; but
the worſt is, the Doĉtor does not *know* your life;
nor can I tell indeed who does, except Dr. Taylor
of Ashbourne. "Why Taylor (said he) is better
acquainted with my *heart* than any man or woman
now alive; and the hiſtory of my Oxford exploits
lies all between him and Adams; but Dr. James
knows my very early days better than he. After
my coming to London to drive the world about a
little, you muſt all go to Jack Hawkesworth for

anecdotes: I lived in great familiarity with him (though I think there was not much affection) from the year 1753 till the time Mr. Thrale and you took me up. I intend, however, to disappoint the rogues, and either make you write the life, with Taylor's intelligence; or, which is better, do it myself, after outliving you all. I am now (added he), keeping a diary, in hopes of using it for that purpose some time." Here the conversation stopped, from my accidentally looking in an old magazine of the year 1768, where I saw the following lines with his name to them, and asked if they were his.

VERSES *said to be written by* Dr. SAMUEL JOHNSON, *at the request of a Gentleman to whom a Lady had given a Sprig of Myrtle.*

WHAT hopes, what terrors, does thy gift create,
Ambiguous emblem of uncertain fate:
The Myrtle, ensign of supreme command,
Consign'd by Venus to Melissa's hand;
Not less capricious than a reigning fair,
Now grants, and now rejects a lover's prayer.
In myrtle shades oft sings the happy swain,
In myrtle shades despairing ghosts complain:
The myrtle crowns the happy lovers' heads,
Th' unhappy lover's grave the myrtle spreads:
O then the meaning of thy gift impart,
And ease the throbbings of an anxious heart!
Soon must this bough, as you shall fix his doom,
Adorn Philander's head, or grace his tomb.

"Why now, do but see how the world is gaping for a wonder! (cries Mr. Johnson;) I think it is now just forty years ago that a young fellow had a sprig of myrtle given him by a girl he courted, and asked me to write him some verses that he might present her in return. I promised, but forgot; and when he called for his lines at the time agreed on—Sit still a moment (says I), dear Mund, and I'll fetch them thee—so stepped aside for five minutes, and wrote the nonsense you now keep such a stir about."

Upon revising these Anecdotes, it is impossible not to be struck with shame and regret that one treasured no more of them up; but no experience is sufficient to cure the vice of negligence: whatever one sees constantly, or might see constantly, becomes uninteresting; and we suffer every trivial occupation, every slight amusement, to hinder us from writing down, what indeed we cannot chuse but remember; but what we should wish to recollect with pleasure, unpoisoned by remorse for not remembering more. While I write this, I neglect impressing my mind with the wonders of art, and beauties of nature, that now surround me; and shall one day, perhaps, think on the hours I might have profitably passed in the Florentine Gallery, and reflecting on Raphael's St. John at that time, as upon Johnson's conversation in this moment, may justly exclaim of the months spent by me most delightfully in Italy—

> That I priz'd every hour that pass'd by,
>   Beyond all that had pleas'd me before;
> But now they are past, and I sigh,
>   And I grieve that I priz'd them no more.
>   SHENSTONE.

Dr. Johnson delighted in his own partiality for Oxford; and one day, at my house, entertained five members of the other university with various inſtances of the superiority of Oxford, enumerating the gigantic names of many men whom it had produced, with apparent triumph. At laſt I said to him, Why there happens to be no less than five Cambridge men in the room now. "I did not (ſaid he) think of that till you told me; but the wolf don't count the sheep." When the company were retired, we happened to be talking of Dr. Barnard, the Provoſt of Eton, who died about that time; and after a long and juſt eulogium on his wit, his learning, and his goodness of heart: "He was the only man too (says Mr. Johnson quite seriously) that did juſtice to my good breeding; and you may observe that I am well-bred to a degree of needless scrupulosity. No man, (continued he, not observing the amazement of his hearers) no man is so cautious not to interrupt another; no man thinks it so necessary to appear attentive when others are speaking; no man so ſteadily refuses preference to himself, or so willingly beſtows it on another, as I do; no body holds so ſtrongly as I do the necessity of ceremony, and the ill effeċts which follow the breach of it: yet people think me rude; but Barnard did me juſtice." 'Tis pity, said I, laughing, that he had not heard you compliment the Cambridge men after dinner to-day. "Why (replied he) I was inclined to *down* them sure enough; but then a

fellow *deserves* to be of Oxford that talks so." I
have heard him at other times relate how he used
to sit in some coffee-house there, and turn M——'s
C-r-ct-u-s into ridicule for the diversion of himself
and of chance comers-in. "The Elf—da (says he)
was too exquisitely pretty; I could make no fun
out of that." When upon some occasions he would
express his astonishment that he should have an
enemy in the world, while he had been doing
nothing but good to his neighbours, I used to
make him recollect these circumstances: "Why
child (said he), what harm could that do the fellow?
I always thought very well of M——n for a *Cambridge* man; he is, I believe, a mighty blameless
character." Such tricks were, however, the more
unpardonable in Mr. Johnson, because no one
could harangue like him about the difficulty always
found in forgiving petty injuries, or in provoking
by needless offence. Mr. Jordan, his tutor, had
much of his affection, though he despised his want
of scholastic learning. "That creature would (said
he) defend his pupils to the last: no young lad
under his care should suffer for committing slight
improprieties, while he had breath to defend, or
power to protect them. If I had had sons to send
to college (added he), Jordan should have been
their tutor."

Sir William Browne the physician, who lived to
a very extraordinary age, and was in other respects
an odd mortal, with more genius than understand-

ing, and more self-sufficiency than wit, was the
only person who ventured to oppose Mr. Johnson,
when he had a mind to shine by exalting his
favourite university, and to express his contempt of
the whiggish notions which prevail at Cambridge.
He did it once, however, with surprising felicity:
his antagonist having repeated with an air of
triumph the famous epigram written by Dr. Trapp,

> Our royal master saw, with heedful eyes,
> The wants of his two universities:
> Troops he to Oxford sent, as knowing why
> That learned body wanted loyalty:
> But books to Cambridge gave, as, well discerning,
> That that right loyal body wanted learning.

Which, says Sir William, might well be answered
thus:

> The king to Oxford sent his troop of horse,
> For Tories own no argument but force;
> With equal care to Cambridge books he sent,
> For Whigs allow no force but argument.

Mr. Johnson did him the justice to say, it was
one of the happiest extemporaneous productions
he ever met with; though he once comically confessed, that he hated to repeat the wit of a whig
urged in support of whiggism. Says Garrick to
him one day, Why did not you make me a tory,
when we lived so much together, you love to make
people tories? "Why (says Johnson, pulling a
heap of halfpence from his pocket) did not the
king make these guineas?"

Of Mr. Johnson's toryism the world has long been witness, and the political pamphlets written by him in defence of his party, are vigorous and elegant. He often delighted his imagination with the thoughts of having destroyed Junius, an anonymous writer who flourished in the years 1769 and 1770, and who kept himself so ingeniously concealed from every endeavour to detect him, that no probable guess was, I believe, ever formed concerning the author's name, though at that time the subject of general conversation. Mr. Johnson made us all laugh one day, because I had received a remarkably fine Stilton cheese as a present from some person who had packed and directed it carefully, but without mentioning whence it came. Mr. Thrale, desirous to know who we were obliged to, asked every friend as they came in, but no body owned it: "Depend upon it, Sir (says Johnson), it was sent by *Junius.*"

The False Alarm, his first and favourite pamphlet, was written at our house between eight o'clock on Wednesday night and twelve o'clock on Thursday night; we read it to Mr. Thrale when he came very late home from the House of Commons: the other political tracts followed in their order. I have forgotten which contains the stroke at Junius; but shall for ever remember the pleasure it gave him to have written it. It was however in the year 1775 that Mr. Edmund Burke made the famous speech in parliament, that struck even foes with admiration, and friends with delight. Among the nameless thousands who are contented to echo those praises they have not skill to invent, *I* ventured, before Dr. Johnson himself, to applaud, with rapture, the beautiful passage in it concerning Lord Bathurst and the Angel; which, said our Doctor, had I been in the house, I would have answered *thus:*

"Suppose, Mr. Speaker, that to Wharton, or to Marlborough, or to any of the eminent whigs of the last age, the devil had, not with any great impropriety, consented to appear; he would perhaps in somewhat like these words have commenced the conversation:

"You seem, my Lord, to be concerned at the judicious apprehension, that while you are sapping the foundations of royalty at home, and propagating here the dangerous doctrine of resistance; the distance of America may secure its inhabitants from your arts, though active: but I will unfold to you the gay prospects of futurity. This people, now so innocent and harmless, shall draw the sword against their mother country, and bathe its point in the blood of their benefactors: this people, now contented with a little, shall then refuse to spare what they themselves confess they could not miss; and these men, now so honest and so grateful, shall, in return for peace and for protection, see their vile agents in the house of parliament, there to sow the seeds of sedition, and propagate confusion, perplexity, and pain. Be not dispirited then

at the contemplation of their present happy state:
I promise you that anarchy, poverty, and death
shall, by my care, be carried even across the
spacious Atlantic, and settle in America itself, the
sure consequences of our beloved whiggism."

This I thought a thing so very particular, that
I begged his leave to write it down directly, before
any thing could intervene that might make me
forget the force of the expressions: a trick, which
I have however seen played on common occasions,
of sitting steadily down at the other end of the
room to write at the moment what should be said
in company, either *by* Dr. Johnson or *to* him, I
never practised myself, nor approved of in another.
There is something so ill-bred, and so inclining to
treachery in this conduct, that were it commonly
adopted, all confidence would soon be exiled from
society, and a conversation assembly-room would
become tremendous as a court of justice. A set of
acquaintance joined in familiar chat may say a
thousand things, which (as the phrase is) pass well
enough at the time, though they cannot stand the
test of critical examination; and as all talk beyond
that which is necessary to the purposes of actual
business is a kind of game, there will be ever found
ways of playing fairly or unfairly at it, which
distinguish the gentleman from the juggler. Dr.
Johnson, as well as many of my acquaintance,
knew that I kept a common-place book; and he one
day said to me good-humouredly, that he would

give me something to write in my repository. "I warrant (said he) there is a great deal about me in it: you shall have at least one thing worth your pains; so if you will get the pen and ink, I will repeat to you Anacreon's Dove directly; but tell at the same time, that as I never was struck with any thing in the Greek language till I read *that*, so I never read any thing in the same language since, that pleased me as much. I hope my translation (continued he) is not worse than that of Frank Fawkes." Seeing me disposed to laugh, "Nay, nay (said he), Frank Fawkes has done them very finely."

Lovely courier of the sky,
Whence and whither dost thou fly?
Scatt'ring, as thy pinions play,
Liquid fragrance all the way:
Is it business? is it love?
Tell me, tell me, gentle Dove.

"Soft Anacreon's vows I bear,
"Vows to Myrtale the fair;
"Grac'd with all that charms the heart,
"Blushing nature, smiling art.
"Venus, courted by an ode,
"On the bard her Dove bestow'd.
"Vested with a master's right
"Now Anacreon rules my flight:
"His the letters that you see,
"Weighty charge consign'd to me:
"Think not yet my service hard,
"Joyless talk without reward:
"Smiling at my master's gates,
"Freedom my return awaits;

"But the liberal grant in vain
"Tempts me to be wild again:
"Can a prudent Dove decline
"Blissful bondage such as mine?
"Over hills and fields to roam,
"Fortune's guest without a home;
"Under leaves to hide one's head,
"Slightly shelter'd, coarsely fed;
"Now my better lot bestows
"Sweet repast, and soft repose;
"Now the generous bowl I sip
"As it leaves Anacreon's lip;
"Void of care, and free from dread,
"From his fingers snatch his bread,
"Then with luscious plenty gay,
"Round his chamber dance and play;
"Or from wine as courage springs,
"O'er his face extend my wings;
"And when feast and frolic tire,
"Drop asleep upon his lyre.
"This is all, be quick and go,
"More than all thou canst not know;
"Let me now my pinions ply,
"I have chatter'd like a pye."

When I had finished, "But you must remember
to add (says Mr. Johnson) that though these verses
were planned, and even begun, when I was sixteen
years old, I never could find time to make an end
of them before I was sixty-eight."

This facility of writing, and this dilatoriness
ever to write, Mr. Johnson always retained, from
the days that he lay a-bed and dictated his first
publication to Mr. Hector, who acted as his

amanuensis, to the moment he made me copy out those variations in Pope's Homer which are printed in the Poets Lives: "And now (said he, when I had finished it for him) I fear not Mr. Nichols of a pin."—The fine Rambler on the subject of Procrastination was hastily composed, as I have heard, in Sir Joshua Reynolds's parlour, while the boy waited to carry it to press: and numberless are the instances of his writing under immediate pressure of importunity or distress. He told me that the character of *Sober* in the Idler, was by himself intended as his own portrait; and that he had his own outset into life in his eye when he wrote the eastern story of Gelaleddin. Of the allegorical papers in the Rambler, Labour and Rest was his favourite; but Serotinus, the man who returns late in life to receive honours in his native country, and meets with mortification instead of respect, was by him considered as a masterpiece in the science of life and manners. The character of Prospero in the fourth volume, Garrick took to be his; and I have heard the author say, that he never forgave the offence. Sophron was likewise a picture drawn from reality; and by Gelidus the philosopher, he meant to represent Mr. Coulson, a mathematician, who formerly lived at Rochester. The man immortalised for purring like a cat was, as he told me, one Busby, a proctor in the Commons. He who barked so ingeniously, and then called the drawer to drive away the dog, was father to

Dr. Salter of the Charterhouse. He who sung a song, and by correspondent motions of his arm chalked out a giant on the wall, was one Richardson, an attorney. The letter signed Sunday, was written by Miss Talbot; and he fancied the billets in the first volume of the Rambler, were sent him by Miss Mulso, now Mrs. Chapone. The papers contributed by Mrs. Carter, had much of his esteem, though he always blamed me for preferring the letter signed Chariessa to the allegory, where religion and superstition are indeed most masterly delineated.

When Dr. Johnson read his own satire, in which the life of a scholar is painted, with the various obstructions thrown in his way to fortune and to fame, he burst into a passion of tears one day: the family and Mr. Scott only were present, who, in a jocose way, clapped him on the back, and said, What's all this, my dear Sir? Why you, and I, and *Hercules*, you know, were all troubled with *melancholy*. As there are many gentlemen of the same name, I should say, perhaps, that it was a Mr. Scott who married Miss Robinson, and that I think I have heard Mr. Thrale call him George Lewis, or George Augustus, I have forgot which. He was a very large man, however, and made out the triumvirate with Johnson and Hercules comically enough. The Doctor was so delighted at his odd sally, that he suddenly embraced him, and the subject was immediately changed. I never saw Mr. Scott but that once in my life.

Dr. Johnson was liberal enough in granting
literary assistance to others, I think; and in-
numerable are the prefaces, sermons, lectures, and
dedications which he used to make for people who
begged of him. Mr. Murphy related in his and
my hearing one day, and he did not deny it, that
when Murphy joked him the week before for
having been so diligent of late between Dodd's
sermon and Kelly's prologue, that Dr. Johnson
replied, "Why, Sir, when they come to me with
a dead stay-maker and a dying parson, what can
a man do?" He *said*, however, that "he hated to
give away literary performances, or even to sell
them too cheaply: the next generation shall not
accuse me (added he) of beating down the price
of literature: one hates, besides, ever to give that
which one has been accustomed to sell; would not
you, Sir (turning to Mr. Thrale), rather give away
money than porter?"

Mr. Johnson had never, by his own account,
been a close student, and used to advise young
people never to be without a book in their pocket,
to be read at bye-times when they had nothing
else to do. "It has been by that means (said he to
a boy at our house one day) that all my knowledge
has been gained, except what I have picked up
by running about the world with my wits ready to
observe, and my tongue ready to talk. A man is
seldom in a humour to unlock his book-case, set
his desk in order, and betake himself to serious

ftudy; but a retentive memory will do something, and a fellow shall have ftrange credit given him, if he can but recollect ftriking passages from different books, keep the authors separate in his head, and bring his ftock of knowledge artfully into play: How else (added he) do the gamefters manage when they play for more money than they are worth?" His Dictionary, however, could not, one would think, have been written by running up and down; but he really did not consider it as a great performance; and used to say, "that he might have done it easily in two years, had not his health received several shocks during the time."

When Mr. Thrale, in consequence of this declaration, teized him in the year 1768 to give a new edition of it, because (said he) there are four or five gross faults: "Alas, Sir (replied Johnson), there are four or five hundred faults, inftead of four or five; but you do not consider that it would take me up three whole months labour, and when the time was expired, the work would not be done." When the booksellers set him about it however some years after, he went cheerfully to the business, said he was well paid, and that they deserved to have it done carefully. His reply to the person who complimented him on its coming out firft, mentioning the ill success of the French in a similar attempt, is well known; and, I truft, has been often recorded: "Why, what would you expect, dear Sir (said he), from fellows that eat frogs?" I have however often thought Dr. Johnson more free than prudent in professing so loudly his little skill in the Greek language: for though he considered it as a proof of a narrow mind to be too careful of literary reputation, yet no man could be more enraged than he, if an enemy, taking advantage of this confession, twitted him with his ignorance; and I remember when the king of Denmark was in England, one of his noblemen was brought by Mr. Colman to see Dr. Johnson at our country-house; and having heard, he said, that he was not famous for Greek literature, attacked him on the weak side; politely adding, that he chose that conversation on purpose to favour himself. Our Doctor, however, displayed so copious, so compendious a knowledge of authors, books, and every branch of learning in that language, that the gentleman appeared astonished. When he was gone home (says Johnson), "Now for all this triumph, I may thank Thrale's Xenophon here, as, I think, excepting that *one*, I have not looked in a Greek book these ten years; but see what haste my dear friends were all in (continued he) to tell this poor innocent foreigner that I knew nothing of Greek! Oh, no, he knows nothing of Greek!" with a loud burst of laughing.

When Davies printed the Fugitive Pieces without his knowledge or consent; How, said I, would Pope have raved, had he been served so? "We should never (replied he) have heard the last on't, to be sure; but then Pope was a narrow man: I will however (added he) storm and bluster *myself* a little this time;"—so went to London in all the wrath he could muster up. At his return I asked how the affair ended: "Why (said he), I was a fierce fellow, and pretended to be very angry, and Thomas was a good-natured fellow, and pretended to be very sorry: so *there* the matter ended: I believe the dog loves me dearly. Mr. Thrale (turning to my husband), what shall you and I do that is good for Tom Davies? We will do something for him, to be sure."

Of Pope as a writer he had the highest opinion, and once when a young lady at our house talked of his preface to Shakespeare as superior to Pope's: "I fear not, Madam (said he), the little fellow has done wonders." His superior reverence of Dryden notwithstanding still appeared in his talk as in his writings; and when some one mentioned the ridicule thrown on him in the Rehearsal, as having hurt his general character as an author: "On the contrary (says Mr. Johnson), the greatness of Dryden's reputation is now the only principle of vitality which keeps the duke of Buckingham's play from putrefaction."

It was not very easy however for people not quite intimate with Dr. Johnson, to get exactly his opinion of a writer's merit, as he would now and then divert himself by confounding those who thought themselves obliged to say to-morrow what

he had said yesterday; and even Garrick, who ought
to have been better acquainted with his tricks,
professed himself mortified, that one time when
he was extolling Dryden in a rapture that I suppose disgusted his friend, Mr. Johnson suddenly
challenged him to produce twenty lines in a series
that would not disgrace the poet and his admirer.
Garrick produced a passage that he had once heard
the Doctor commend, in which he *now* found, if I
remember rightly, sixteen faults, and made Garrick
look silly at his own table. When I told Mr. Johnson the story, "Why, what a monkey was David
now (says he), to tell of his own disgrace!" And in
the course of that hour's chat he told me, how he
used to teize Garrick by commendations of the
tomb scene in Congreve's Mourning Bride, protesting that Shakespeare had in the same line of
excellence nothing as good: "All which is strictly
true (said he); but that is no reason for supposing
Congreve is to stand in competition with Shakespeare: these fellows know not how to blame, nor
how to commend." I forced him one day, in a
similar humour, to prefer Young's description of
Night to the so much admired ones of Dryden and
Shakespeare, as more forcible, and more general.
Every reader is not either a lover or a tyrant, but
every reader is interested when he hears that

> Creation sleeps; 'tis as the general pulse
> Of life stood still, and nature made a pause;
> An awful pause—prophetic of its end.

"This (said he) is true; but remember that taking the compositions of Young in general, they are but like bright stepping-stones over a miry road: Young froths, and foams, and bubbles sometimes very vigorously; but we must not compare the noise made by your tea-kettle here with the roaring of the ocean."

Somebody was praising Corneille one day in opposition to Shakespeare: "Corneille is to Shakespeare (replied Mr. Johnson) as a clipped hedge is to a forest." When we talked of Steele's Essays, "They are too thin (says our Critic) for an Englishman's taste: mere superficial observations on life and manners, without erudition enough to make them keep, like the light French wines, which turn sour with standing a while for want of *body*, as we call it."

Of a much admired poem, when extolled as beautiful (he replied), "That it had indeed the beauty of a bubble: the colours are gay (said he), but the substance slight." Of James Harris's Dedication to his Hermes I have heard him observe, that, though but fourteen lines long, there were six grammatical faults in it. A friend was praising the style of Dr. Swift; Mr. Johnson did not find himself in the humour to agree with him: the critic was driven from one of his performances to the other. At length you *must* allow me, said the gentleman, that there are *strong facts* in the account of the Four last Years of Queen Anne: "Yes surely

Sir (replies Johnson), and so there are in the Ordinary of Newgate's account." This was like the story which Mr. Murphy tells, and Johnson always acknowledged: How Dr. Rose of Chiswick, contending for the preference of Scotch writers over the English, after having set up his authors like nine-pins, while the Doctor kept bowling them down again; at last, to make sure of victory, he named Ferguson upon Civil Society, and praised the book for being written in a *new* manner. "I do not (says Johnson) perceive the value of this new manner; it is only like Buckinger, who had no hands, and so wrote with his feet." Of a modern Martial when it came out: "There are in these verses (says Dr. Johnson) too much folly for madness, I think, and too much madness for folly." If, however, Mr. Johnson lamented, that the nearer he approached to his own times, the more enemies he should make, by telling biographical truths in his Lives of the later Poets, what may I not apprehend, who, if I relate anecdotes of Mr. Johnson, am obliged to repeat expressions of severity, and sentences of contempt? Let me at least soften them a little, by saying, that he did not hate the persons he treated with roughness, or despise them whom he drove from him by apparent scorn. He really loved and respected many whom he would not suffer to love him. And when he related to me a short dialogue that passed between himself and a writer of the first eminence in the world, when he was in Scotland, I was shocked to think how he must have disgusted him. Dr. ———— asked me (said he) why I did not join in their public worship when among them? for (said he) I went to your churches often when in England. "So (replied Johnson) I have read that the Siamese sent ambassadors to Louis Quatorze, but I never heard that the king of France thought it worth his while to send ambassadors from his court to that of *Siam*." He was no gentler with myself, or those for whom I had the greatest regard. When I one day lamented the loss of a first cousin killed in America————"Prithee, my dear (said he), have done with canting: how would the world be worse for it, I may ask, if all your relations were at once spitted like larks, and roasted for Presto's supper?" Presto was the dog that lay under the table while we talked.————When we went into Wales together, and spent some time at Sir Robert Cotton's at Lleweny, one day at dinner I meant to please Mr. Johnson particularly with a dish of very young peas. Are not they charming? said I to him, while he was eating them.—"Perhaps (said he) they would be so—to a *pig*." I only instance these replies, to excuse my mentioning those he made to others.

When a well-known author published his poems in the year 1777: Such a one's verses are come out, said I: "Yes (replied Johnson), and this frost has struck them in again. Here are some lines I have written to ridicule them: but remember that I love the fellow dearly, now—for all I laugh at him.

> Wheresoe'er I turn my view,
> All is strange, yet nothing new:
> Endless labour all along,
> Endless labour to be wrong;
> Phrase that Time has flung away;
> Uncouth words in disarray,
> Trick'd in antique ruff and bonnet,
> Ode, and elegy, and sonnet."

When he parodied the verses of another eminent writer, it was done with more provocation, I believe, and with some merry malice. A serious translation of the same lines, which I think are from Euripides, may be found in Burney's History of Music.—Here are the burlesque ones:

> Err shall they not, who resolute explore
> Times gloomy backward with judicious eyes;
> And scanning right the practices of yore,
> Shall deem our hoar progenitors unwise.
>
> They to the dome where smoke with curling play
> Announc'd the dinner to the regions round,
> Summon'd the singer blythe, and harper gay,
> And aided wine with dulcet-streaming sound.
>
> The better use of notes, or sweet or shrill,
> By quiv'ring string, or modulated wind;
> Trumpet or lyre—to their harsh bosoms chill,
> Admission ne'er had sought, or could not find.
>
> Oh! send them to the sullen mansions dun,
> Her baleful eyes where Sorrow rolls around;
> Where gloom-enamour'd Mischief loves to dwell,
> And Murder, all blood-bolter'd, schemes the wound.

> When cates luxuriant pile the spacious dish,
> And purple nectar glads the festive hour;
> The guest, without a want, without a wish,
> Can yield no room to Music's soothing pow'r.

Some of the old lengendary stories put in verse by modern writers provoked him to caricature them thus one day at Streatham; but they are already well-known, I am sure.

> The tender infant, meek and mild,
>   Fell down upon the stone;
> The nurse took up the squealing child,
>   But still the child squeal'd on.

A famous ballad also, beginning *Rio verde, Rio verde*, when I commended the translation of it, he said he could do it better himself—as thus:

> Glassy water, glassy water,
> Down whose current clear and strong,
> Chiefs confus'd in mutual slaughter,
> Moor and Christian roll along.

But Sir, said I, this is not ridiculous at all. "Why no (replied he), why should I always write ridiculously?—perhaps because I made these verses to imitate such a one, naming him:

> Hermit hoar, in solemn cell,
> Wearing out life's evening gray;
> Strike thy bosom sage! and tell,
> What is bliss, and which the way?
>
> Thus I spoke, and speaking sigh'd,
> Scarce repress'd the starting tear,
> When the hoary Sage reply'd,
> Come, my lad, and drink some beer."

I could give another comical instance of caricatura imitation. Recollecting some day, when praising these verses of Lopez de Vega,

> *Se a quien los leones vence*
> *Vence una muger hermosa*
> *O el de flaco averguençe*
> *O ella di ser mas furiosa,*

more than he thought they deserved, Mr. Johnson instantly observed, "that they were founded on a trivial conceit; and that conceit ill-explained, and ill-expressed beside.——The lady, we all know, does not conquer in the same manner as the lion does: 'Tis a mere play of words (added he), and you might as well say, that

> If the man who turnips cries,
> Cry not when his father dies,
> 'Tis a proof that he had rather
> Have a turnip than his father."

And this humour is of the same sort with which he answered the friend who commended the following line:

> Who rules o'er freemen should himself be free.

"To be sure (said Dr. Johnson),

> Who drives fat oxen should himself be fat."

This readiness of finding a parallel, or making one, was shewn by him perpetually in the course of conversation.—When the French verses of a certain pantomime were quoted thus,

> *Je suis Cassandre descendüe des cieux,*
> *Pour vous fair entendre, mesdames et messieurs,*
> *Que je suis Cassandre descendüe des cieux;*

he cried out gaily and suddenly, almost in a moment,

> "I am Cassandra come down from the sky,
> To tell each by-ſtander what none can deny,
> That I am Cassandra come down from the sky."

The pretty Italian verses too, at the end of Baretti's book, called "Easy Phraseology," he did *all' improviso*, in the same manner:

> *Viva! viva la padrona!*
> *Tutta bella, e tutta buona,*
> *La padrona è un angiolella*
> *Tutta buona e tutta bella;*
> *Tutta bella e tutta buona;*
> *Viva! viva la padrona!*

> Long may live my lovely Hetty!
> Always young and always pretty,
> Always pretty, always young,
> Live my lovely Hetty long!
> Always young and always pretty;
> Long may live my lovely Hetty!

The famous diſtich too, of an Italian *improvisatore*, who, when the duke of Modena ran away from the comet in the year 1742 or 1743,

> *Se al venir veſtro i principi sen' vanno*
> *Deh venga ogni di——durate un anno;*

"which (said he) would do juſt as well in our language thus:

> If at your coming princes disappear,
> Comets! come every day—and ſtay a year."

When some one in company commended the verses of M. de Benserade *à son Lit*;

Théatre des ris et des pleurs,
Lit! où je nais, et où je meurs,
Tu nous fais voir comment voisins,
Sont nos plaisirs, et nos chagrins.

To which he replied without hesitating,

"In bed we laugh, in bed we cry,
And born in bed, in bed we die;
The near approach a bed may shew,
Of human bliss to human woe."

The inscription on the collar of Sir Joseph Banks's goat which had been on two of his adventurous expeditions with him, and was then, by the humanity of her amiable master, turned out to graze in Kent, as a recompence for her utility and faithful service, was given me by Johnson in the year 1777 I think, and I have never yet seen it printed.

Perpetui, ambitâ bis terrâ, premia lactis,
Hæc habet altrici Capra secunda Jovis.

The epigram written at Lord Anson's house many years ago, "where (says Mr. Johnson) I was well received and kindly treated, and with the true gratitude of a wit ridiculed the master of the house before I had left it an hour," has been falsely printed in many papers since his death. I wrote it down from his own lips one evening in August 1772, not neglecting the little preface, accusing himself of making so graceless a return for the civilities shewn him. He had, among other elegancies about the park and gardens, been made to observe a temple to the winds, when this thought naturally presented itself *to a wit.*

> *Gratum animum laudo; Qui debuit omnia ventis,*
> *Quam bene ventorum, surgere templa jubet!*

A translation of Dryden's epigram too, I used to fancy I had to myself.

> *Quos laudet vates, Graius, Romanus, et Anglus,*
> *Tres tria temporibus secla dedere suis:*
> *Sublime ingenium Graius,—Romanus habebat*
> *Carmen grande sonans, Anglus utrumque tulit.*
> *Nil majus natura capit; clarare priores*
> *Quæ potuere duos, tertius unus habet:*

from the famous lines written under Milton's picture:

> Three poets in three distant ages born,
> Greece, Italy, and England did adorn;
> The first in loftiness of thought surpast,
> The next in majesty; in both the last.
> The force of Nature could no further go,
> To make a third she join'd the former two.

One evening in the oratorio season of the year 1771, Mr. Johnson went with me to Covent-Garden theatre; and though he was for the most part an exceedingly bad playhouse companion, as his person drew people's eyes upon the box, and the loudness of his voice made it difficult for me to hear any body but himself; he sat surprisingly quiet, and I flattered myself that he was listening to the music. When we were got home however he repeated these verses, which he said he had made at the oratorio, and he bid me translate them.

IN THEATRO.

Tertii verso quater orbe luStri
Quid theatrales tibi Crispe pompæ!
Quam decet canos male literatos
                    Sera voluptas!

Tene mulceri fidibus canoris?
Tene cantorum modulis Stupere?
Tene per piĉtas oculo elegante
                    Currere formas?

Inter equales sine felle liber,
Codices veri Studiosus inter
Reĉtius vives, sua quisque carpat
                    Gaudia gratus.

Lusibus gaudet puer otiosis
Luxus obleĉtat juvenem theatri,
At seni fluxo sapienter uti
                    Tempora reStat.

I gave him the following lines in imitation, which
he liked well enough, I think:

When threescore years have chill'd thee quite,
Still can theatric scenes delight?
Ill suits this place with learned wight,
          May Bates or Coulson cry.

The scholar's pride can Brent disarm?
His heart can soft Guadagni warm?
Or scenes with sweet delusion charm
          The climaĉteric eye?

The social club, the lonely tower,
Far better suit thy midnight hour;
Let each according to his power
          In worth or wisdom shine!

And while play pleases idle boys,
And wanton mirth fond youth employs,
To fix the soul, and free from toys,
    That useful task be thine.

The copy of verses in Latin hexameters, as well as I remember, which he wrote to Dr. Lawrence, I forgot to keep a copy of; and he obliged me to resign his translation of the song beginning, *Busy, curious, thirsty fly*, for him to give Mr. Langton, with a promise *not* to retain a copy. I concluded he knew why, so never enquired the reason. He had the greatest possible value for Mr. Langton, of whose virtue and learning he delighted to talk in very exalted terms; and poor Dr. Lawrence had long been his friend and confident. The conversation I saw them hold together in Essex-street one day in the year 1781 or 1782, was a melancholy one, and made a singular impression on my mind. He was himself exceedingly ill, and I accompanied him thither for advice. The physician was however, in some respects, more to be pitied than the patient: Johnson was panting under an asthma and dropsy; but Lawrence had been brought home that very morning struck with the palsy, from which he had, two hours before we came, strove to awaken himself by blisters: they were both deaf, and scarce able to speak besides; one from difficulty of breathing, the other from paralytic debility. To give and receive medical counsel therefore, they fairly sate down on each side a table in the Doctor's gloomy apartment, adorned with skeletons, preserved monsters, &c. and agreed to write Latin billets to each other: such a scene did I never see! "You (said Johnson) are *timidè* and *gelidè*;" finding that his friend had prescribed palliative not drastic remedies. It is not *me*, replies poor Lawrence in an interrupted voice; 'tis nature that is *gelidè* and *timidè*. In fact he lived but few months after I believe, and retained his faculties still a shorter time. He was a man of strict piety and profound learning, but little skilled in the knowledge of life or manners, and died without having ever enjoyed the reputation he so justly deserved.

Mr. Johnson's health had been always extremely bad since I first knew him, and his over-anxious care to retain without blemish the perfect sanity of his mind, contributed much to disturb it. He had studied medicine diligently in all its branches; but had given particular attention to the diseases of the imagination, which he watched in himself with a solicitude destructive of his own peace, and intolerable to those he trusted. Dr. Lawrence told him one day, that if he would come and beat him once a week he would bear it; but to hear his complaints was more than *man* could support. 'Twas therefore that he tried, I suppose, and in eighteen years contrived to weary the patience of a *woman*. When Mr. Johnson felt his fancy, or fancied he felt it, disordered, his constant recurrence was to the study of arithmetic; and one day that he was totally confined to his chamber, and I enquired what he had been doing to divert himself; he shewed me a calculation which I could scarce be made to understand, so vast was the plan of it, and so very intricate were the figures: no other indeed than that the national debt, computing it at one hundred and eighty millions sterling, would, if converted into silver, serve to make a meridian of that metal, I forget how broad, for the globe of the whole earth, the real *globe*. On a similar occasion I asked him (knowing what subject he would like best to talk upon), How his opinion stood towards the question between Paschal and Soame Jennings about number and numeration? as the French philosopher observes that infinity, though on all sides astonishing, appears most so when the idea is connected with the idea of number; for the notions of infinite number, and infinite number we know there is, stretches one's capacity still more than the idea of infinite space; "Such a notion indeed (adds he) can scarcely find room in the human mind." Our English author on the other hand exclaims, let no man give himself leave to talk about infinite number, for infinite number is a contradiction in terms; whatever is once numbered, we all see cannot be infinite. "I think (said Mr. Johnson after a pause) we must settle the matter thus: numeration is certainly infinite, for eternity might be employed in adding unit to unit; but every number is in itself finite, as the possibility of doubling it easily proves: besides, ſtop at what point you will, you find yourself as far from infinitude as ever." These passages I wrote down as soon as I had heard them, and repent that I did not take the same method with a dissertation he made one other day that he was very ill, concerning the peculiar properties of the number Sixteen, which I afterwards tried, but in vain, to make him repeat.

As ethics or figures, or metaphysical reasoning, was the sort of talk he moſt delighted in, so no kind of conversation pleased him less I think, than when the subjeᴄt was hiſtorical faᴄt or general polity. "What shall we learn from *that* ſtuff (said he)? let us not fancy like Swift that we are exalting a woman's charaᴄter by telling how she

> Could name the ancient heroes round,
> Explain for what they were renown'd, &c."

I muſt not however lead my readers to suppose that he meant to reserve such talk for *men's* company as a proof of pre-eminence. "He never (as he expressed it) desired to hear of the *Punic war* while he lived: such conversation was loſt time (he said), and carried one away from common life, leaving no ideas behind which would serve *living wight* as warning or direᴄtion."

> How I should aᴄt is not the case,
> But how would Brutus in my place?

"And now (cries Mr. Johnson, laughing with obſtreperous violence), if these two foolish lines can be equalled in folly, except by the two succeeding ones—shew them me."

I asked him once concerning the conversation powers of a gentleman with whom I was myself unacquainted—"He talked to me at club one day (replies our Doctor) concerning Catiline's conspiracy—so I withdrew my attention, and thought about Tom Thumb."

Modern politics fared no better. I was one time extolling the character of a ſtatesman, and expatiating on the skill required to direct the different currents, reconcile the jarring intereſts, &c. "Thus (replies he) a mill is a complicated piece of mechanism enough, but the water is no part of the workmanship."——On another occasion, when some one lamented the weakness of a then present miniſter, and complained that he was dull and tardy, and knew little of affairs,—"You may as well complain, Sir (says Johnson), that the accounts of time are kept by the clock; for he certainly does ſtand ſtill upon the ſtair-head—and we all know that he is no great chronologer."——In the year 1777, or thereabouts, when all the talk was of an invasion, he said moſt pathetically one afternoon, "Alas! alas! how this unmeaning ſtuff spoils all my comfort in my friends conversation! Will the people never have done with it; and shall I never hear a sentence again without the *French* in it?

Here is no invasion coming, and you *know* there is none. Let the vexatious and frivolous talk alone, or suffer it at least to teach you *one* truth; and learn by this perpetual echo of even unapprehended distress, how historians magnify events expected, or calamities endured; when you know they are at this very moment collecting all the big words they can find, in which to describe a consternation never felt, for a misfortune which never happened. Among all your lamentations, who eats the less? Who sleeps the worse, for one general's ill success, or another's capitulation? *Oh, pray* let us hear no more of it!"——No man however was more zealously attached to his party; he not only loved a tory himself, but he loved a man the better if he heard he hated a whig. "Dear Bathurst (said he to me one day) was a man to my very heart's content: he hated a fool, and he hated a rogue, and he hated a *whig*; he was a very good *hater*."

Some one mentioned a gentleman of that party for having behaved oddly on an occasion where faction was not concerned:—"Is he not a citizen of London, a native of North America, and a whig? (says Johnson)—Let him be absurd, I beg of you: when a monkey is *too* like a man, it shocks one."

Severity towards the poor was, in Dr. Johnson's opinion (as is visible in his Life of Addison particularly), an undoubted and constant attendant or consequence upon whiggism; and he was not contented with giving them relief, he wished to add

also indulgence. He loved the poor as I never yet
saw any one else do, with an earnest desire to make
them happy.—What signifies, says some one,
giving halfpence to common beggars? they only
lay it out in gin or tobacco. "And why should they
be denied such sweeteners of their existence (says
Johnson)? it is surely very savage to refuse them
every possible avenue to pleasure, reckoned too
coarse for our own acceptance. Life is a pill which
none of us can bear to swallow without gilding;
yet for the poor we delight in stripping it still barer,
and are not ashamed to shew even visible dis-
pleasure, if ever the bitter taste is taken from their
mouths." In consequence of these principles he
nursed whole nests of people in his house, where
the lame, the blind, the sick, and the sorrowful
found a sure retreat from all the evils whence his
little income could secure them: and commonly
spending the middle of the week at our house, he
kept his numerous family in Fleet-street upon a
settled allowance; but returned to them every
Saturday, to give them three good dinners, and his
company, before he came back to us on the Monday
night——treating them with the same, or perhaps
more ceremonious civility, than he would have
done by as many people of fashion——making the
holy scriptures thus the rule of his conduct, and
only expecting salvation as he was able to obey its
precepts.

While Dr. Johnson possessed however the

ſtrongeſt compassion for poverty or illness, he did not even pretend to feel for those who lamented the loss of a child, a parent, or a friend.——"These are the diſtresses of sentiment (he would reply) which a man who is really to be pitied has no leisure to feel. The sight of people who want food and raiment is so common in great cities, that a surly fellow like me, has no compassion to spare for wounds given only to vanity or softness." No man, therefore, who smarted from the ingratitude of his friends, found any sympathy from our philosopher: "Let him do good on higher motives next time," would be the answer; "he will then be sure of his reward."——It is easy to observe, that the juſtice of such sentences made them offensive; but we muſt be careful how we condemn a man for saying what we know to be true, only because it *is* so. I hope that the reason our hearts rebelled a little againſt his severity, was chiefly because it came from a living mouth.——Books were invented to take off the odium of immediate superiority, and soften the rigour of duties prescribed by the teachers and censors of human kind—setting at leaſt those who are acknowledged wiser than ourselves at a diſtance. When we recolleſt however, that for this very reason *they* are seldom consulted and little obeyed, how much cause shall his contemporaries have to rejoice that their living Johnson forced them to feel the reproofs due to vice and folly—while Seneca and Tillotson were no longer able to make impression—except on our shelves. Few things indeed which pass well enough with others would do with him: he had been a great reader of Mandeville, and was ever on the watch to spy out those stains of original corruption, so easily discovered by a penetrating observer even in the purest minds. I mentioned an event, which if it had happened would greatly have injured Mr. Thrale and his family——and then, dear Sir, said I, how sorry you would have been! "I *hope* (replied he after a long pause)—I should have been *very* sorry;——but remember Rochefoucault's maxim."——I would rather (answered I) remember Prior's verses, and ask,

> What need of books these truths to tell,
> Which folks perceive that cannot spell?
> And must we spectacles apply,
> To see what hurts our naked eye?

Will *any* body's mind bear this eternal microscope that you place upon your own so? "I never (replied he) saw one that *would*, except that of my dear Miss Reynolds—and her's is very near to purity itself."——Of slighter evils, and friends less distant than our own household, he spoke less cautiously. An acquaintance lost the almost certain hope of a good estate that had been long expected. Such a one will grieve (said I) at her friend's disappointment. "She will suffer as much perhaps (said he) as your horse did when your cow miscarried."——I professed myself sincerely grieved when accumulated distresses crushed Sir George Colebrook's family; and I was so. "Your own prosperity (said he) may possibly have so far increased the natural tenderness of your heart, that for aught I know you *may* be a *little sorry*; but it is sufficient for a plain man if he does not laugh when he sees a fine new house tumble down all on a sudden, and a snug cottage stand by ready to receive the owner, whose birth entitled him to nothing better, and whose limbs are left him to go to work again with."

I used to tell him in jest, that his morality was easily contented; and when I have said something as if the wickedness of the world gave me concern, he would cry out aloud against canting, and protest that he thought there was very little gross wickedness in the world, and still less of extraordinary virtue. Nothing indeed more surely disgusted Dr. Johnson than hyperbole; he loved not to be told of sallies of excellence, which he said were seldom valuable, and seldom true. "Heroic virtues (said he) are the *bons mots* of life; they do not appear often, and when they do appear are too much prized I think; like the aloe-tree, which shoots and flowers once in a hundred years. But life is made up of little things; and that character is the best which does little but repeated acts of beneficence; as that conversation is the best which consists in elegant and pleasing thoughts expressed in natural and pleasing terms. With regard to my own notions

of moral virtue (continued he), I hope I have not
lost my sensibility of wrong; but I hope likewise
that I have lived long enough in the world, to
prevent me from expecting to find any action of
which both the original motive and all the parts
were good."

The piety of Dr. Johnson was exemplary and
edifying: he was punctiliously exact to perform
every public duty enjoined by the church, and his
spirit of devotion had an energy that affected all
who ever saw him pray in private. The coldest and
most languid hearers of the word must have felt
themselves animated by his manner of reading the
holy scriptures; and to pray by his sick bed, required strength of body as well as of mind, so
vehement were his manners, and his tones of voice
so pathetic. I have many times made it my request
to heaven that I might be spared the sight of his
death; and I was spared it!

Mr. Johnson, though in general a gross feeder,
kept fast in Lent, particularly the holy week, with
a rigour very dangerous to his general health; but
though he had left off wine (for religious motives
as I always believed, though he did not own it),
yet he did not hold the commutation of offences
by voluntary penance, or encourage others to
practise severity upon themselves. He even once
said, "that he thought it an error to endeavour at
pleasing God by taking the rod of reproof out of
his hands." And when we talked of convents, and

the hardships suffered in them—"Remember always (said he) that a convent is an idle place, and where there is nothing to be *done* something must be *endured:* mustard has a bad taste *per se* you may observe, but very insipid food cannot be eaten without it."

His respect however for places of religious retirement was carried to the greatest degree of earthly veneration: the Benedictine convent at Paris paid him all possible honours in return, and the Prior and he parted with tears of tenderness. Two of that college being sent to England on the mission some years after, spent much of their time with him at Bolt Court I know, and he was ever earnest to retain their friendship; but though beloved by all his Roman Catholic acquaintance, particularly Dr. Nugent, for whose esteem he had a singular value, yet was Mr. Johnson a most unshaken church of England man; and I think, or at least I once *did* think, that a letter written by him to Mr. Barnard the King's librarian, when he was in Italy collecting books, contained some very particular advice to his friend to be on his guard against the seductions of the church of Rome.

The settled aversion Dr. Johnson felt towards an infidel he expressed to all ranks, and at all times, without the smallest reserve; for though on common occasions he paid great deference to birth or title, yet his regard for truth and virtue never gave way to meaner considerations. We talked of a dead wit one evening, and somebody praised him—"Let us never praise talents so ill employed, Sir; we foul our mouths by commending such infidels (said he)." Allow him the *lumières* at least, intreated one of the company—"I do allow him, Sir (replied Johnson), just enough to light him to hell."——Of a Jamaica gentleman, then lately dead—"He will not, whither he is now gone (said Johnson), find much difference, I believe, either in the climate or the company."——The Abbé Reynal probably remembers that, being at the house of a common friend in London, the master of it approached Johnson with that gentleman so much celebrated in his hand, and this speech in his mouth: Will you permit me, Sir, to present to you the Abbé Reynal? "*No, Sir*," (replied the Doctor very loud) and suddenly turned away from them both.

Though Mr. Johnson had but little reverence either for talents or fortune, when he found them unsupported by virtue; yet it was sufficient to tell him a man was very pious, or very charitable, and he would at least *begin* with him on good terms, however the conversation might end. He would, sometimes too, good-naturedly enter into a long chat for the instruction or entertainment of people he despised. I perfectly recollect his condescending to delight my daughter's dancing-master with a long argument about *his* art; which the man protested, at the close of the discourse, the Doctor knew more of than himself; who remained astonished, enlightened, and amused by the talk of a person little likely to make a good disquisition upon dancing. I have sometimes indeed been rather pleased than vexed when Mr. Johnson has given a rough answer to a man who perhaps deserved one only half as rough, because I knew he would repent of his hasty reproof, and make us all amends by some conversation at once instructive and entertaining, as in the following cases: A young fellow asked him abruptly one day, Pray, Sir, what and where is Palmira? I heard somebody talk last night of the ruins of Palmira. "'Tis a hill in Ireland (replies Johnson), with palms growing on the top, and a bog at the bottom, and so they call it *Palm-mira*." Seeing however that the lad thought him serious, and thanked him for the information, he undeceived him very gently indeed; told him the history, geography, and chronology of Tadmor in the wilderness, with every incident that literature could furnish I think, or eloquence express, from the building of Solomon's palace to the voyage of Dawkins and Wood.

On another occasion, when he was musing over the fire in our drawing-room at Streatham, a young gentleman called to him suddenly, and I suppose he thought disrespectfully, in these words: Mr. Johnson, Would you advise me to marry? "I would advise no man to marry, Sir (returns for answer in a very angry tone Dr. Johnson), who is not likely to propagate understanding;" and so left the room. Our companion looked confounded, and I believe had scarce recovered the consciousness of his own existence, when Johnson came back, and drawing his chair among us, with altered looks and a softened voice, joined in the general chat, insensibly led the conversation to the subject of marriage, where he laid himself out in a dissertation so useful, so elegant, so founded on the true knowledge of human life, and so adorned with beauty of sentiment, that no one ever recollected the offence, except to rejoice in its consequences. He repented just as certainly however, if he had been led to praise any person or thing by accident more than he thought it deserved; and was on such occasions comically earnest to destroy the praise or pleasure he had unintentionally given.

Sir Joshua Reynolds mentioned some picture as excellent. "It has often grieved me, Sir (said Mr. Johnson), to see so much mind as the science of painting requires, laid out upon such perishable materials: why do not you oftener make use of copper? I could wish your superiority in the art you profess, to be preserved in stuff more durable than canvas." Sir Joshua urged the difficulty of procuring a plate large enough for historical subjects, and was going to raise further objections: "What foppish obstacles are these! (exclaims on a sudden Dr. Johnson:) Here is Thrale has a thousand tun of copper; you may paint it all round if you will, I suppose; it will serve him to brew in afterwards: Will it not, Sir?" (to my husband who sat by.) Indeed Dr. Johnson's utter scorn of painting was such, that I have heard him say, that he should sit very quietly in a room hung round with the works of the greatest masters, and never feel the slightest disposition to turn them if their backs were outermost, unless it might be for the sake of telling Sir Joshua that he *had* turned them. Such speeches may appear offensive to many, but those who knew he was too blind to discern the perfections of an art which applies itself immediately to our eye-sight, must acknowledge he was not in the wrong.

He delighted no more in music than painting; he was almost as deaf as he was blind: travelling with Dr. Johnson was for these reasons tiresome enough. Mr. Thrale loved prospects, and was mortified that his friend could not enjoy the sight of those different dispositions of wood and water, hill and valley, that travelling through England and France affords a man. But when he wished to point them out to his companion: "Never heed such nonsense," would be the reply: "a blade of grass is always a blade of grass, whether in one country or another: let us if we *do* talk, talk about something; men and women are my subjects of enquiry; let us see how these differ from those we have left behind."

When we were at Rouen together, he took a great fancy to the Abbé Roffette, with whom he

conversed about the destruction of the order of
Jesuits, and condemned it loudly, as a blow to the
general power of the church, and likely to be
followed with many and dangerous innovations,
which might at length become fatal to religion
itself, and shake even the foundation of Christianity.
The gentleman seemed to wonder and delight in
his conversation: the talk was all in Latin, which
both spoke fluently, and Mr. Johnson pronounced
a long eulogium upon Milton with so much ardour,
eloquence, and ingenuity, that the Abbé rose from
his seat and embraced him. My husband seeing
them apparently so charmed with the company of
each other, politely invited the Abbé to England,
intending to oblige his friend; who, instead of
thanking, reprimanded him severely before the
man, for such a sudden burst of tenderness towards
a person he could know nothing at all of; and thus
put a sudden finish to all his own and Mr. Thrale's
entertainment from the company of the Abbé
Roffette.

When at Versailles the people shewed us the
theatre. As we stood on the stage looking at some
machinery for playhouse purposes: Now we are
here, what shall we act, Mr. Johnson,—The
Englishman at Paris? "No, no (replied he), we
will try to act Harry the Fifth." His dislike of the
French was well known to both nations, I believe;
but he applauded the number of their books and
the graces of their style. "They have few senti-

ments (said he), but they express them neatly; they have little meat too, but they dress it well." Johnson's own notions about eating however were nothing less than delicate; a leg of pork boiled till it dropped from the bone, a veal-pye with plums and sugar, or the outside cut of a salt buttock of beef, were his favourite dainties: with regard to drink, his liking was for the strongest, as it was not the flavour, but the effect he sought for, and professed to desire; and when I first knew him, he used to pour capillaire into his Port wine. For the last twelve years however, he left off all fermented liquors. To make himself some amends indeed, he took his chocolate liberally, pouring in large quantities of cream, or even melted butter; and was so fond of fruit, that though he usually eat seven or eight large peaches of a morning before breakfast began, and treated them with proportionate attention after dinner again, yet I have heard him protest that he never had quite as much as he wished of wall-fruit, except once in his life, and that was when we were all together at Ombersley, the seat of my Lord Sandys. I was saying to a friend one day, that I did not like goose; one smells it so while it is roasting, said I: "But you, Madam (replies the Doctor), have been at all times a fortunate woman, having always had your hunger so forestalled by indulgence, that you never experienced the delight of smelling your dinner beforehand." Which pleasure, answered I pertly, is to be enjoyed in perfection by such as have the happiness to pass through Porridge-Island * of a morning. "Come, come (says he gravely), let's have no sneering at what is serious to so many: hundreds of your fellow-creatures, dear Lady, turn another way, that they may not be tempted by the luxuries of Porridge-Island to wish for gratifications they are not able to obtain: you are certainly not better than all of *them*; give God thanks that you are happier."

I received on another occasion as just a rebuke from Mr. Johnson, for an offence of the same nature, and hope I took care never to provoke a third; for after a very long summer particularly hot and dry, I was wishing naturally but thoughtlessly for some rain to lay the dust as we drove along the Surry roads. "I cannot bear (replied he, with much asperity and an altered look), when I know how many poor families will perish next winter for want of that bread which the present drought will deny them, to hear ladies sighing for rain, only that their complexions may not suffer from the heat, or their clothes be incommoded by the dust;—for shame! leave off such foppish lamentations, and study to relieve those whose distresses are real."

With advising others to be charitable however,

* Porridge-Island is a mean street in London, filled with cook-shops for the convenience of the poorer inhabitants; the real name of it I know not, but suspect that it is generally known by, to have been originally a term of derision.

Dr. Johnson did not content himself. He gave away all he had, and all he ever had gotten, except the two thousand pounds he left behind; and the very small portion of his income which he spent on himself, with all our calculation, we never could make more than seventy, or at moſt fourscore pounds a year, and he pretended to allow himself a hundred. He had numberless dependents out of doors as well as in, "who, as he expressed it, did not like to see him latterly unless he brought 'em money." For those people he used frequently to raise contributions on his richer friends; "and this (says he) is one of the thousand reasons which ought to reſtrain a man from drony solitude and useless retirement. Solitude (added he one day) is dangerous to reason, without being favourable to virtue: pleasures of some sort are necessary to the intelleᶜtual as to the corporeal health; and those who resiſt gaiety, will be likely for the moſt part to fall a sacrifice to appetite; for the solicitations of sense are always at hand, and a dram to a vacant and solitary person is a speedy and seducing relief. Remember (continued he) that the solitary mortal is certainly luxurious, probably superſtitious, and possibly mad: the mind ſtagnates for want of employment, grows morbid, and is extinguished like a candle in foul air." It was on this principle that Johnson encouraged parents to carry their daughters early and much into company: "for what harm can be done before so many witnesses?

Solitude is the surest nurse of all prurient passions, and a girl in the hurry of preparation, or tumult of gaiety, has neither inclination nor leisure to let tender expressions soften or sink into her heart. The ball, the show, are not the dangerous places: no, 'tis the private friend, the kind consoler, the companion of the easy vacant hour, whose compliance with her opinions can flatter her vanity, and whose conversation can just sooth, without ever stretching her mind, that is the lover to be feared: he who buzzes in her ear at court, or at the opera, must be contented to buzz in vain." These notions Dr. Johnson carried so very far, that I have heard him say, "if you would shut up any man with any woman, so as to make them derive their whole pleasure from each other, they would inevitably fall in love, as it is called, with each other; but at six months end if you would throw them both into public life where they might change partners at pleasure, each would soon forget that fondness which mutual dependance, and the paucity of general amusement alone, had caused, and each would separately feel delighted by their release."

In these opinions Rousseau apparently concurs with him exactly; and Mr. Whitehead's poem called *Variety*, is written solely to elucidate this simple proposition. Prior likewise advises the husband to send his wife abroad, and let her see the world as it really stands——

> Powder, and pocket-glass, and beau.

Mr. Johnson was indeed unjuſtly supposed to be a lover of singularity. Few people had a more settled reverence for the world than he, or was less captivated by new modes of behaviour introduced, or innovations on the long-received cuſtoms of common life. He hated the way of leaving a company without taking notice to the lady of the house that he was going; and did not much like any of the contrivances by which ease has been lately introduced into society inſtead of ceremony, which had more of his approbation. Cards, dress, and dancing however, all found their advocates in Dr. Johnson, who inculcated, upon principle, the cultivation of those arts, which many a moraliſt thinks himself bound to rejeƈt, and many a Chriſtian holds unfit to be praƈtised. "No person (said he one day) goes under-dressed till he thinks himself of consequence enough to forbear carrying the badge of his rank upon his back." And in answer to the arguments urged by Puritans, Quakers, &c. againſt showy decorations of the human figure, I once heard him exclaim, "Oh, let us not be found when our Maſter calls us, ripping the lace off our waiſtcoats, but the spirit of contention from our souls and tongues! Let us all conform in outward cuſtoms, which are of no consequence, to the manners of those whom we live among, and despise such paltry diſtinƈtions. Alas, Sir (continued he), a man who cannot get to heaven in a green coat, will not find his way thither the sooner in a grey one." On an occasion of less consequence, when he turned his back on Lord Bolingbroke in the rooms at Brighthelmstone, he made this excuse: "I am not obliged, Sir (said he to Mr. Thrale, who stood fretting), to find reasons for respecting the rank of him who will not condescend to declare it by his dress or some other visible mark: what are stars and other signs of superiority made for?"

The next evening however he made us comical amends, by sitting by the same nobleman, and haranguing very loudly about the nature and use and abuse of divorces. Many people gathered round them to hear what was said, and when my husband called him away, and told him to whom he had been talking—received an answer which I will not write down.

Though no man perhaps made such rough replies as Dr. Johnson, yet nobody had a more just aversion to general satire; he always hated and censured Swift for his unprovoked bitterness against the professors of medicine; and used to challenge his friends, when they lamented the exorbitancy of physicians fees, to produce him one instance of an estate raised by physic in England. When an acquaintance too was one day exclaiming against the tediousness of the law and its partiality; "Let us hear, Sir (said Johnson), no general abuse; the law is the last result of human wisdom acting upon human experience for the benefit of the public."

As the mind of Dr. Johnson was greatly expanded, so his first care was for general, not particular or petty morality; and those teachers had more of his blame than praise, I think, who seek to oppress life with unnecessary scruples: "Scruples would (as he observed) certainly make men miserable, and seldom make them good. Let us ever (he said) studiously fly from those instructors against whom our Saviour denounces heavy judgments, for having bound up burdens grievous to be borne, and laid them on the shoulders of mortal men." No one had however higher notions of the hard task of true Christianity than Johnson, whose daily terror lest he had not done enough, originated in piety, but ended in little less than disease. Reasonable with regard to others, he had formed vain hopes of performing impossibilities himself; and finding his good works ever below his desires and intent, filled his imagination with fears that he should never obtain forgiveness for omissions of duty and criminal waste of time. These ideas kept him in constant anxiety concerning his salvation; and the vehement petitions he perpetually made for a longer continuance on earth, were doubtless the cause of his so prolonged existence; for when I carried Dr. Pepys to him in the year 1782, it appeared wholly impossible for any skill of the physician or any strength of the patient to save him. He was saved that time however by Sir Lucas's prescriptions; and less skill on one side, or less ſtrength on the other, I am morally certain, would not have been enough. He had however possessed an athletic conſtitution, as he said the man who dipped people in the sea at Brighthelm-ſtone acknowledged; for seeing Mr. Johnson swim in the year 1766, Why Sir (says the dipper), you muſt have been a ſtout-hearted gentleman forty years ago.

Mr. Thrale and he used to laugh about that ſtory very often: but Garrick told a better, for he said that in their young days, when some ſtrolling players came to Litchfield, our friend had fixed his place upon the ſtage, and got himself a chair accordingly; which leaving for a few minutes, he found a man in it at his return, who refused to give it back at the firſt intreaty: Mr. Johnson however, who did not think it worth his while to make a second, took chair and man and all together, and threw them all at once into the pit. I asked the Doctor if this was a faſt? "Garrick has not *spoiled* it in the telling (said he), it is very *near* true to be sure."

Mr. Beauclerc too related one day, how on some occasion he ordered two large maſtiffs into his parlour, to shew a friend who was conversant in canine beauty and excellence, how the dogs quarrelled, and faſtening on each other, alarmed all the company except Johnson, who seizing one in one hand by the cuff of the neck, the other in the other hand, said gravely, "Come, gentlemen! where's your difficulty? put one dog out at the door, and I will shew this fierce gentleman the way out of the window:" which, lifting up the maſtiff and the sash, he contrived to do very expeditiously, and much to the satisfaction of the affrighted company. We inquired as to the truth of this curious recital. "The dogs have been somewhat magnified, I believe Sir (was the reply): they were, as I remember, two ſtout young pointers; but the ſtory has gained but little."

One reason why Mr. Johnson's memory was so particularly exact, might be derived from his rigid attention to veracity; being always resolved to relate every fact as it ſtood, he looked even on the smaller parts of life with minute attention, and remembered such passages as escape cursory and common observers. "A ſtory (says he) is a specimen of human manners, and derives its sole value from its truth. When Foote has told me something, I dismiss it from my mind like a passing shadow: when Reynolds tells me something, I consider myself as possessed of an idea the more."

Mr. Johnson liked a frolic or a jeſt well enough; though he had ſtrange serious rules about it too: and very angry was he if any body offered to be merry when he was disposed to be grave. "You have an ill-founded notion (said he) that it is clever to turn matters off with a joke (as the phrase is); whereas nothing produces enmity so certain, as one person's shewing a disposition to be merry when another is inclined to be either serious or displeased."

One may gather from this how he felt, when his Irish friend Grierson, hearing him enumerate the qualities necessary to the formation of a poet, began a comical parody upon his ornamented harangue in praise of a cook, concluding with this observation, that he who dressed a good dinner was a more excellent and a more useful member of society than he who wrote a good poem. "And in this opinion (said Mr. Johnson in reply) all the dogs in the town will join you."

Of this Mr. Grierson I have heard him relate many droll stories, much to his advantage as a wit, together with some facts more difficult to be accounted for; as avarice never was reckoned among the vices of the laughing world. But Johnson's various life, and spirit of vigilance to learn and treasure up every peculiarity of manner, sentiment, or general conduct, made his company, when he chose to relate anecdotes of people he had formerly known, exquisitely amusing and comical. It is indeed inconceivable what strange occurrences he had seen, and what surprising things he could tell when in a communicative humour. It is by no means my business to relate memoirs of his acquaintance; but it will serve to shew the character of Johnson himself, when I inform those who never knew him, that no man told a story with so good a grace, or knew so well what would make an effect upon his auditors. When he raised contributions for some distressed author, or wit in want, he often made us all more than amends by diverting descriptions of the lives they were then passing in

corners unseen by any body but himself and that
odd old surgeon whom he kept in his house to tend
the out-pensioners, and of whom he said moſt truly
and sublimely, that

> In misery's darkeſt caverns known,
>   His useful care was ever nigh,
> Where hopeless anguish pours her groan,
>   And lonely want retires to die.

I have forgotten the year, but it could scarcely
I think be later than 1765 or 1766, that he was
called abruptly from our house after dinner, and
returning in about three hours, said, he had been
with an enraged author, whose landlady pressed
him for payment within doors, while the bailiffs
beset him without; that he was drinking himself
drunk with Madeira to drown care, and fretting
over a novel which when finished was to be his
whole fortune; but he could not get it done for
diſtraction, nor could he ſtep out of doors to offer
it to sale. Mr. Johnson therefore set away the
bottle, and went to the bookseller, recommending
the performance, and desiring some immediate
relief; which when he brought back to the writer,
he called the woman of the house directly to par-
take of punch, and pass their time in merriment.

It was not till ten years after, I dare say, that
something in Dr. Goldsmith's behaviour ſtruck
me with an idea that he was the very man, and
then Johnson confessed that he was so; the novel
was the charming Vicar of Wakefield.

There was a Mr. Boyce too, who wrote some very elegant verses printed in the Magazines of five-and-twenty years ago, of whose ingenuity and distress I have heard Dr. Johnson tell some curious anecdotes; particularly, that when he was almost perishing with hunger, and some money was produced to purchase him a dinner, he got a bit of roast beef, but could not eat it without ketchup, and laid out the last half-guinea he possessed in truffles and mushrooms, eating them in bed too, for want of clothes, or even a shirt to sit up in.

Another man for whom he often begged, made as wild use of his friend's beneficence as these, spending in punch the solitary guinea which had been brought him one morning; when resolving to add another claimant to a share of the bowl, besides a woman who always lived with him, and a footman who used to carry out petitions for charity, he borrowed a chairman's watch, and pawning it for half a crown, paid a clergyman to marry him to a fellow-lodger in the wretched house they all inhabited, and got so drunk over the guinea bowl of punch the evening of his wedding-day, that having many years lost the use of one leg, he now contrived to fall from the top of the stairs to the bottom, and break his arm, in which condition his companions left him to call Mr. Johnson, who relating the series of his tragi-comical distresses, obtained from the Literary Club a seasonable relief.

Of that respectable society I have heard him

speak in the highest terms, and with a magnificent panegyric on each member, when it consisted only of a dozen or fourteen friends; but as soon as the necessity of enlarging it brought in new faces, and took off from his confidence in the company, he grew less fond of the meeting, and loudly proclaimed his carelessness *who* might be admitted, when it was become a mere dinner club. I *think* the original names, when I first heard him talk with fervor of every member's peculiar powers of instructing or delighting mankind, were Sir John Hawkins, Mr. Burke, Mr. Langton, Mr. Beauclerc, Dr. Percy, Dr. Nugent, Dr. Goldsmith, Sir Robert Chambers, Mr. Dyer, and Sir Joshua Reynolds, whom he called their Romulus, or said somebody else of the company called him so, which was more likely: but this was, I believe, in the year 1775 or 1776. It was a supper meeting then, and I fancy Dr. Nugent ordered an omelet sometimes on a Friday or Saturday night; for I remember Mr. Johnson felt very painful sensations at the sight of that dish soon after his death, and cried, "Ah, my poor dear friend! I shall never eat omelet with *thee* again!" quite in an agony. The truth is, nobody suffered more from pungent sorrow at a friend's death than Johnson, though he would suffer no one else to complain of their losses in the same way; "for (says he) we must either outlive our friends you know, or our friends must outlive us; and I see no man that would hesitate about the choice."

Mr. Johnson loved late hours extremely, or more properly hated early ones. Nothing was more terrifying to him than the idea of retiring to bed, which he never would call going to rest, or suffer another to call so. "I lie down (said he) that my acquaintance may sleep; but I lie down to endure oppressive misery, and soon rise again to pass the night in anxiety and pain." By this pathetic manner, which no one ever possessed in so eminent a degree, he used to shock me from quitting his company, till I hurt my own health not a little by sitting up with him when I was myself far from well: nor was it an easy matter to oblige him even by compliance, for he always maintained that no one forbore their own gratifications for the sake of pleasing another, and if one *did* sit up it was probably to amuse one's self. Some right however he certainly had to say so, as he made his company exceedingly entertaining when he had once forced one, by his vehement lamentations and piercing reproofs, not to quit the room, but to sit quietly and make tea for him, as I often did in London till four o'clock in the morning. At Streatham indeed I managed better, having always some friend who was kind enough to engage him in talk, and favour my retreat.

The first time I ever saw this extraordinary man was in the year 1764, when Mr. Murphy, who had been long the friend and confidential intimate of Mr. Thrale, persuaded him to wish for Johnson's conversation, extolling it in terms which that of no other person could have deserved, till we were only in doubt how to obtain his company, and find an excuse for the invitation. The celebrity of Mr. Woodhouse a shoemaker, whose verses were at that time the subject of common discourse, soon afforded a pretence, and Mr. Murphy brought Johnson to meet him, giving me general cautions not to be surprised at his figure, dress, or behaviour. What I recollect best of the day's talk, was his earnestly recommending Addison's works to Mr. Woodhouse as a model for imitation. "Give nights and days, Sir (said he), to the study of Addison, if you mean either to be a good writer, or what is more worth, an honest man." When I saw something like the same expression in his criticism on that author, lately published, I put him in mind of his past injunctions to the young poet, to which he replied, "That he wished the shoemaker might have remembered them as well." Mr. Johnson liked his new acquaintance so much however, that from that time he dined with us every Thursday through the winter, and in the autumn of the next year he followed us to Brighthelmstone, whence we were gone before his arrival; so he was disappointed and enraged, and wrote us a letter expressive of anger, which we were very desirous to pacify, and to obtain his company again if possible. Mr. Murphy brought him back to us again very kindly, and from that time his visits grew more frequent, till in the year 1766 his health, which he had always complained of, grew so exceedingly bad, that he could not ſtir out of his room in the court he inhabited for many *weeks* together, I think *months*.

Mr. Thrale's attentions and my own now became so acceptable to him, that he often lamented to us the horrible condition of his mind, which he said was nearly diſtraĉted; and though he charged *us* to make him odd solemn promises of secrecy on so ſtrange a subjeĉt, yet when we waited on him one morning, and heard him, in the moſt pathetic terms, beg the prayers of Dr. Delap, who had left him as we came in, I felt excessively affeĉted with grief, and well remember my husband involuntarily lifted up one hand to shut his mouth, from provocation at hearing a man so wildly proclaim what he could at laſt persuade no one to believe; and what, if true, would have been so very unfit to reveal.

Mr. Thrale went away soon after, leaving me with him, and bidding me prevail on him to quit his close habitation in the court and come with us to Streatham, where I undertook the care of his health, and had the honour and happiness of contributing to its reſtoration. This task, though diſtressing enough sometimes, would have been less so had not my mother and he disliked one another extremely, and teized me often with perverse opposition, petty contentions, and mutual complaints. Her superfluous attention to such accounts of the foreign politics as are transmitted to us by the daily prints, and her willingness to

talk on subjects he could not endure, began the
aversion; and when, by the peculiarity of his style,
she found out that he teized her by writing in the
newspapers concerning battles and plots which had
no existence, only to feed her with new accounts of
the division of Poland perhaps, or the disputes
between the states of Russia and Turkey, she was
exceedingly angry to be sure, and scarcely I think
forgave the offence till the domestic distresses of
the year 1772 reconciled them to and taught them
the true value of each other; excellent as *they both*
were, far beyond the excellence of any other man
and woman I ever yet saw. As her conduct too
extorted his truest esteem, her cruel illness excited
all his tenderness; nor was the sight of beauty,
scarce to be subdued by disease, and wit, flashing
through the apprehension of evil, a scene which
Dr. Johnson could see without sensibility. He
acknowledged himself improved by her piety, and
astonished at her fortitude, and hung over her bed
with the affection of a parent, and the reverence
of a son. Nor did it give me less pleasure to see
her sweet mind cleared of all its latent prejudices,
and left at liberty to admire and applaud that force
of thought and versatility of genius, that comprehensive soul and benevolent heart which attracted
and commanded veneration from all, but inspired
peculiar sensations of delight mixed with reverence
in those who, like her, had the opportunity to
observe these qualities, stimulated by gratitude,

and actuated by friendship. When Mr. Thrale's perplexities disturbed his peace, dear Dr. Johnson left him scarce a moment, and tried every artifice to amuse as well as every argument to console him: nor is it more possible to describe than to forget his prudent, his pious attentions towards the man who had some years before certainly saved his valuable life, perhaps his reason, by half obliging him to change the foul air of Fleet-street for the wholesome breezes of the Sussex Downs.

The epitaph engraved on my mother's monument shews how deserving she was of general applause. I asked Johnson why he named her person before her mind: he said it was, "because every body could judge of the one, and but few of the other."

Juxta sepulta est HESTERA MARIA
Thomæ Cotton de Combermere baronetti Cestriensis filia,
Johannis Salusbury armigeri Flintiensis uxor.
Forma felix, felix ingenio;
Omnibus jucunda, suorum amantissima.
Linguis artibusque ita exculta
Ut loquenti nunquam deessent
Sermonis nitor, sententiarum flosculi,
Sapientiæ gravitas, leporum gratia
Modum servandi adeo perita,
Ut domestica inter negotia literis oblectaretur.
Literarum inter delicias, rem familiarem sedulo curaret,
Multis illi multos annos precantibus
diri carcinomatis veneno contabuit,
nexibusque vitæ paulatim resolutis,
è terris—meliora sperans—emigravit.
Nata 1707. *Nupta* 1739. *Obiit* 1773.

Mr. Murphy, who admired her talents and delighted in her company, did me the favour to paraphrase this elegant inscription in verses which I fancy have never yet been published. His fame has long been out of my power to increase as a poet; as a man of sensibility perhaps these lines may set him higher than he now stands. I remember with gratitude the friendly tears which prevented him from speaking as he put them into my hand.

Near this place
Are deposited the remains of
HESTER MARIA,
The daughter of Sir Thomas Cotton of Combermere, in the county of Cheshire, Bart. the wife of
John Salusbury,
of the county of Flint, Esquire. She was
born in the year 1707, married in 1739, and died
in 1773.

A pleasing form, where every grace combin'd,
With genius blest, a pure enlighten'd mind;
Benevolence on all that smiles bestow'd,
A heart that for her friends with love o'erflow'd:
In language skill'd, by science form'd to please,
Her mirth was wit, her gravity was ease.
Graceful in all, the happy mien she knew,
Which even to virtue gives the limits due;
Whate'er employ'd her, that she seem'd to chuse,
Her house, her friends, her business, or the muse.
Admir'd and lov'd, the theme of general praise,
All to such virtue wish'd a length of days;
But sad reverse! with slow-consuming pains,
Th' envenom'd cancer revell'd in her veins;

Prey'd on her spirits—ſtole each power away;
Gradual she sunk, yet smiling in decay;
She smil'd in hope, by sore afflictions try'd,
And in that hope the pious Chriſtian died.

The following epitaph on Mr. Thrale, who has
now a monument close by her's in Streatham
church, I have seen printed and commended in
Maty's Review for April 1784; and a friend has
favoured me with a translation.

Hic conditur quod reliquum eſt
HENRICI THRALE,
Qui res seu civiles, seu domeſticas, ita egit,
Ut vitam illi longiorem multi optarent;
Ita sacras,
Ut quam brevem esset habiturus præscire videretur;
Simplex, apertus, sibique semper similis,
Nihil oſtentavit aut arte fiſtum aut cura
Elaboratum.
In senatu, regi patriæque
Fideliter ſtuduit;
Vulgi obſtrepentis contemptor animosus,
Domi inter mille mercaturæ negotia
Literarum elegantiam minimè neglexit.
Amicis quocunque modo laborantibus,
Conciliis, auſtoritate, muneribus adfuit.
Inter familiares, comites, convivas, hospites,
Tam facili fuit morum suavitate
Ut omnium animos ad se alliceret;
Tam felici sermonis libertate
Ut nulli adulatus, omnibus placeret.
Natus 1724. Ob. 1781.
Consortes tumuli habet Rodolphum patrem, ſtrenuum
fortemque virum, et Henricum filium unicum,
quem spei parentum mors inopina decennem
præripuit.

Ita
Domus felix et opulenta, quam erexit
Avus, auxitque pater, cum nepote decidit.
Abi viator!
Et vicibus rerum humanarum perspectis,
Æternitatem cogita!

Here are deposited the remains of
HENRY THRALE,
Who managed all his concerns in the present
world, public and private, in such a manner
as to leave many wishing he had continued
longer in it;
And all that related to a future world,
as if he had been sensible how short a time he
was to continue in this.
Simple, open, and uniform in his manners,
his conduct was without either art or affectation.
In the senate steadily attentive to the true interests
of his king and country,
He looked down with contempt on the clamours
of the multitude:
Though engaged in a very extensive business,
He found some time to apply to polite literature:
And was ever ready to assist his friends
labouring under any difficulties,
with his advice, his influence, and his purse.
To his friends, acquaintance, and guests,
he behaved with such sweetness of manners
as to attach them all to his person:
So happy in his conversation with them,
as to please all, though he flattered none.
He was born in the year 1724, and died in 1781.
In the same tomb lie interred his father
Ralph Thrale, a man of vigour and activity,
And his only son Henry, who died before his father,
Aged ten years.

> Thus a happy and opulent family,
> Raised by the grandfather, and augmented by the
> father, became extinguished with the grandson.
> Go, Reader,
> And reflecting on the vicissitudes of
> all human affairs,
> Meditate on eternity.

I never recollect to have heard that Dr. Johnson wrote inscriptions for any sepulchral stones, except Dr. Goldsmith's in Westminster abbey, and these two in Streatham church. He made four lines once, on the death of poor Hogarth, which were equally true and pleasing: I know not why Garrick's were preferred to them.

> The hand of him here torpid lies,
> That drew th' essential form of grace;
> Here clos'd in death th' attentive eyes,
> That saw the manners in the face.

Mr. Hogarth, among the variety of kindnesses shewn to me when I was too young to have a proper sense of them, was used to be very earnest that I should obtain the acquaintance, and if possible the friendship of Dr. Johnson, whose conversation was to the talk of other men, like Titian's painting compared to Hudson's, he said: but don't you tell people now, that I say so (continued he), for the connoisseurs and I are at war you know; and because I hate *them*, they think I hate *Titian*—and let them!—Many were indeed the lectures I used to have in my very early days from dear Mr.

Hogarth, whose regard for my father induced him perhaps to take notice of his little girl, and give her some odd particular directions about dress, dancing, and many other matters interesting now only because they were his. As he made all his talents, however, subservient to the great purposes of morality, and the earnest desire he had to mend mankind, his discourse commonly ended in an ethical dissertation, and a serious charge to me, never to forget his picture of the *Lady's last Stake*. Of Dr. Johnson, when my father and he were talking together about him one day: That man (says Hogarth) is not contented with believing the Bible, but he fairly resolves, I think, to believe nothing *but* the Bible. Johnson (added he), though so wise a fellow, is more like king David than king Solomon; for he says in his haste that all men are liars. This charge, as I afterwards came to know, was but too well founded: Mr. Johnson's incredulity amounted almost to disease, and I have seen it mortify his companions exceedingly. But the truth is, Mr. Thrale had a very powerful influence over the Doctor, and could make him suppress many rough answers: he could likewise prevail on him to change his shirt, his coat, or his plate, almost before it came indispensably necessary to the comfortable feelings of his friends: But as I never had any ascendency at all over Mr. Johnson, except just in the things that concerned his health, it grew extremely perplexing and difficult to live

in the house with him when the master of it was
no more; the worse indeed, because his dislikes
grew capricious; and he could scarce bear to have
any body come to the house whom it was absolutely
necessary for me to see. Two gentlemen, I perfectly well remember, dining with us at Streatham
in the Summer 1782, when Elliot's brave defence
of Gibraltar was a subject of common discourse,
one of these men naturally enough begun some
talk about red-hot balls thrown with surprizing
dexterity and effect: which Dr. Johnson having
listened some time to, "I would advise you, Sir
(said he with a cold sneer), never to relate this story
again: you really can scarce imagine how *very poor*
a figure you make in the telling of it." Our guest
being bred a Quaker, and I believe a man of an
extremely gentle disposition, needed no more reproofs for the same folly; so if he ever did speak
again, it was in a low voice to the friend who came
with him. The check was given before dinner, and
after coffee I left the room. When in the evening
however our companions were returned to London,
and Mr. Johnson and myself were left alone, with
only our usual family about us, "I did not quarrel
with those Quaker fellows," (said he, very seriously.)
You did perfectly right, replied I; for they gave
you no cause of offence. "No offence! (returned
he with an altered voice;) and is it nothing then
to sit whispering together when *I* am present,
without ever directing their discourse towards me,

or offering me a share in the conversation?" That was, because you frighted him who spoke first about those hot balls. "Why, Madam, if a creature is neither capable of giving dignity to falsehood, nor willing to remain contented with the truth, he deserves no better treatment."

Mr. Johnson's fixed incredulity of every thing he heard, and his little care to conceal that incredulity, was teizing enough to be sure: and I saw Mr. Sharp was pained exceedingly, when relating the history of a hurricane that happened about that time in the West Indies, where, for aught I know, he had himself lost some friends too, he observed Dr. Johnson believed not a syllable of the account: "For 'tis *so* easy (says he) for a man to fill his mouth with a wonder, and run about telling the lie before it can be detected, that I have no heart to believe hurricanes easily raised by the first inventor, and blown forwards by thousands more." I asked him once if he believed the story of the destruction of Lisbon by an earthquake when it first happened: "Oh! not for six months (said he) at least: I *did* think that story too dreadful to be credited, and can hardly yet persuade myself that it was true to the full extent we all of us have heard."

Among the numberless people however whom I heard him grossly and flatly contradict, I never yet saw any one who did not take it patiently excepting Dr. Burney, from whose habitual softness of manners I little expected such an exertion of spirit: the event was as little to be expected. Mr. Johnson asked his pardon generously and genteelly, and when he left the room rose up to shake hands with him, that they might part in peace. On another occasion, when he had violently provoked Mr. Pepys, in a different but perhaps not a less offensive manner, till something much too like a quarrel was grown up between them, the moment he was gone, "Now (says Dr. Johnson) is Pepys gone home hating me, who love him better than I did before: he spoke in defence of his dead friend; but though I hope *I* spoke better who spoke against him, yet all my eloquence will gain me nothing but an honest man for my enemy!" He did not however cordially love Mr. Pepys, though he respected his abilities. "I knew the dog was a scholar (said he, when they had been disputing about the classics for three hours together one morning at Streatham); but that he had so much taste and so much knowledge I did *not* believe: I might have taken Barnard's word though, for Barnard would not lie."

We had got a little French print among us at Brighthelmstone, in November 1782, of some people skating, with these lines written under:

> *Sur un mince chrystal l'hyver conduit leurs pas,*
> *Le precipice est sous la glace;*
> *Telle est de nos plaisirs la legere surface,*
> *Glissez mortels; n'appuyez pas.*

And I begged translations from every body: Dr. Johnson gave me this;

> O'er ice the rapid skaiter flies,
>> With sport above and death below;
> Where mischief lurks in gay disguise,
>> Thus lightly touch and quickly go.

He was however most exceedingly enraged when he knew that in the course of the season I had asked half a dozen acquaintance to do the same thing, and said, it was a piece of treachery, and done to make every body else look little when compared to my favourite friends the *Pepyses*, whose translations were unquestionably the best. I will insert them, because he *did* say so. This is the distich given me by Sir Lucas, to whom I owe more solid obligations, no less than the power of thanking him for the life he saved, and whose least valuable praise is the correctness of his taste:

> O'er the ice as o'er pleasure you lightly should glide;
> Both have gulphs which their flattering surfaces hide.

This other more serious one was written by his brother:

> Swift o'er the level how the skaiters slide,
>> And skim the glitt'ring surface as they go:
> Thus o'er life's specious pleasures lightly glide,
>> But pause not, press not on the gulph below.

Dr. Johnson seeing this last, and thinking a moment, repeated,

O'er crackling ice, o'er gulphs profound,
  With nimble glide the skaiters play;
O'er treacherous pleasure's flow'ry ground
  Thus lightly skim, and haste away.

Though thus uncommonly ready both to give and take offence, Mr. Johnson had many rigid maxims concerning the necessity of continued softness and compliance of disposition: and when I once mentioned Shenstone's idea, that some little quarrel among lovers, relations, and friends was useful, and contributed to their general happiness upon the whole, by making the soul feel her elastic force, and return to the beloved object with renewed delight:—"Why, what a pernicious maxim is this now (cries Johnson), *all* quarrels ought to be avoided studiously, particularly conjugal ones, as no one can possibly tell where they may end; besides that lasting dislike is often the consequence of occasional disgust, and that the cup of life is surely bitter enough, without squeezing in the hateful rind of resentment." It was upon something like the same principle, and from his general hatred of refinement, that when I told him how Dr. Collier, in order to keep the servants in humour with his favourite dog, by seeming rough with the animal himself on many occasions, and crying out, Why will nobody knock this cur's brains out? meant to conciliate their tenderness towards Pompey; he returned me for answer, "that the maxim was evidently false, and founded on ignorance of

human life: that the servants would kick the dog
the sooner for having obtained such a sanction to
their severity: and I once (added he) chid my wife
for beating the cat before the maid, who will now
(said I) treat puss with cruelty perhaps, and plead
her mistress's example."

I asked him upon this, if he ever disputed with
his wife? (I had heard that he loved her passion-
ately.) "Perpetually (said he): my wife had a
particular reverence for cleanliness, and desired
the praise of neatness in her dress and furniture,
as many ladies do, till they become troublesome to
their best friends, slaves to their own besoms, and
only sigh for the hour of sweeping their husbands
out of the house as dirt and useless lumber: a
clean floor is *so* comfortable, she would say sometimes, by way of twitting; till at last I told her,
that I thought we had had talk enough about
the *floor*, we would now have a touch at the
cieling."

On another occasion I have heard him blame
her for a fault many people have, of setting the
miseries of their neighbours half unintentionally
half wantonly before their eyes, shewing them the
bad side of their profession, situation, &c. He said,
"she would lament the dependence of pupillage
to a young heir, &c. and once told a waterman who
rowed her along the Thames in a wherry, that he
was no happier than a galley-slave, one being
chained to the oar by authority, the other by want.

I had however (said he, laughing), the wit to get
her daughter on my side always before we began
the dispute. She read comedy better than any body
he ever heard (he said); in tragedy she mouthed
too much."

Garrick told Mr. Thrale however, that she was
a little painted puppet, of no value at all, and quite
disguised with affectation, full of odd airs of rural
elegance; and he made out some comical scenes, by
mimicking her in a dialogue he pretended to have
overheard: I do not know whether he meant such
stuff to be believed or no, it was so comical; nor
did I indeed ever see him represent her ridiculously,
though my husband did. The intelligence I gained
of her from old Levett, was only perpetual illness
and perpetual opium. The picture I found of her
at Litchfield was very pretty, and her daughter
Mrs. Lucy Porter said it was like. Mr. Johnson
has told me, that her hair was eminently beautiful,
quite *blonde* like that of a baby; but that she fretted
about the colour, and was always desirous to dye
it black, which he very judiciously hindered her
from doing. His account of their wedding we used
to think ludicrous enough—"I was riding to
church (says Johnson), and she following on another
single horse: she hung back however, and I turned
about to see whether she could get her steed along,
or what was the matter. I had however soon
occasion to see it was only coquetry, and *that I
despised,* so quickening my pace a little, she mended

hers; but I believe there was a tear or two——
pretty dear creature!"

Johnson loved his dinner exceedingly, and has
often said in my hearing, perhaps for my edifica-
tion, "that wherever the dinner is ill got there is
poverty, or there is avarice, or there is stupidity;
in short, the family is somehow grossly wrong: for
(continued he) a man seldom thinks with more
earnestness of any thing than he does of his dinner;
and if he cannot get that well dressed, he should
be suspected of inaccuracy in other things." One
day when he was speaking upon the subject, I asked
him, if he ever huffed his wife about his dinner?
"So often (replied he), that at last she called to me,
and said, Nay, hold Mr. Johnson, and do not make
a farce of thanking God for a dinner which in a
few minutes you will protest not eatable."

When any disputes arose between our married
acquaintance however, Mr. Johnson always sided
with the husband, "whom (he said) the woman
had probably provoked so often, she scarce knew
when or how she had disobliged him first. Women
(says Dr. Johnson) give great offence by a contemptuous spirit of non-compliance on petty occasions. The man calls his wife to walk with him in
the shade, and she feels a strange desire just at that
moment to sit in the sun: he offers to read her a
play, or sing her a song, and she calls the children
in to disturb them, or advises him to seize that
opportunity of settling the family accounts. Twenty

such tricks will the faithfulleſt wife in the world
not refuse to play, and then look aſtonished when
the fellow fetches in a miſtress. Boarding-schools
were eſtablished (continued he) for the conjugal
quiet of the parents: the two partners cannot agree
which child to fondle, nor how to fondle them, so
they put the young ones to school, and remove the
cause of contention. The little girl pokes her head,
the mother reproves her sharply: Do not mind
your mamma, says the father, my dear, but do your
own way. The mother complains to me of this:
Madam (said I), your husband is right all the
while; he is with you but two hours of the day
perhaps, and then you teize him by making the
child cry. Are not ten hours enough for tuition?
And are the hours of pleasure so frequent in life,
that when a man gets a couple of quiet ones to
spend in familiar chat with his wife, they muſt be
poisoned by petty mortifications? Put missey to
school; she will learn to hold her head like her
neighbours, and you will no longer torment your
family for want of other talk."

The vacuity of life had at some early period of
his life ſtruck so forcibly on the mind of Mr. Johnson, that it became by repeated impression his
favourite hypothesis, and the general tenor of his
reasonings commonly ended there, wherever they
might begin. Such things therefore as other philosophers often attribute to various and contradiſtory
causes, appeared to him uniform enough; all was

done to fill up the time, upon his principle. I used to tell him, that it was like the Clown's answer in All's well that ends well, of "Oh Lord, Sir!" for that it suited every occasion. One man, for example, was profligate and wild, as we call it, followed the girls, or sat still at the gaming-table. "Why, life must be filled up (says Johnson), and the man who is not capable of intellectual pleasures must content himself with such as his senses can afford." Another was a hoarder: "Why, a fellow must do something; and what so easy to a narrow mind as hoarding halfpence till they turn into sixpences."—Avarice was a vice against which, however, I never much heard Mr. Johnson declaim, till one represented it to him connected with cruelty, or some such disgraceful companion. "Do not (said he) discourage your children from hoarding, if they have a taste to it: whoever lays up his penny rather than part with it for a cake, at least is not the slave of gross appetite; and shews besides a preference always to be esteemed, of the future to the present moment. Such a mind may be made a good one; but the natural spendthrift, who grasps his pleasures greedily and coarsely, and cares for nothing but immediate indulgence, is very little to be valued above a negro." We talked of Lady Tavistock, who grieved herself to death for the loss of her husband—"She was rich and wanted employment (says Johnson), so she cried till she lost all power of restraining her tears: other women are forced to outlive their husbands, who were just as much beloved, depend on it; but they have no time for grief: and I doubt not, if we had put my Lady Tavistock into a small chandler's shop, and given her a nurse-child to tend, her life would have been saved. The poor and the busy have no leisure for sentimental sorrow." We were speaking of a gentleman who loved his friend—"Make him prime minister (says Johnson) and see how long his friend will be remembered." But he had a rougher answer for me, when I commended a sermon preached by an intimate acquaintance of our own at the trading end of the town. "What was the subject, Madam (says Dr. Johnson)?" Friendship, Sir (replied I). "Why now, is it not strange that a wise man, like our dear little Evans, should take it in his head to preach on such a subject, in a place where no one can be thinking of it?" Why, what are they thinking upon, Sir (said I)? "Why, the men are thinking on their money I suppose, and the women are thinking of their mops."

Dr. Johnson's knowledge and esteem of what we call low or coarse life was indeed prodigious; and he did not like that the upper ranks should be dignified with the name of *the world*. Sir Joshua Reynolds said one day, that nobody *wore* laced coats now; and that once every body wore them. "See now (says Johnson) how absurd that is; as if the bulk of mankind consisted of fine gentlemen that came to him to sit for their pictures. If every man who wears a laced coat (that he can pay for) was extirpated, who would miss them?" With all this haughty contempt of gentility, no praise was more welcome to Dr. Johnson than that which said he had the notions or manners of a gentleman: which character I have heard him define with accuracy, and describe with elegance. "Officers (he said) were falsely supposed to have the carriage of gentlemen; whereas no profession left a stronger brand behind it than that of a soldier; and it was the essence of a gentleman's character to bear the visible mark of no profession whatever." He once named Mr. Berenger as the standard of true elegance; but some one objecting that he too much resembled the gentleman in Congreve's comedies, Mr. Johnson said, "We must fix them upon the famous Thomas Hervey, whose manners were polished even to acuteness and brilliancy, though he lost but little in solid power of reasoning, and in genuine force of mind." Mr. Johnson had however an avowed and scarcely limited partiality for all who bore the name or boasted the alliance of an Aston or a Hervey; and when Mr. Thrale once asked him which had been the happiest period of his past life? he replied, "it was that year in which he spent one whole evening with M——y As——n. That indeed (said he) was not happiness, it was rapture; but the thoughts of it sweetened the whole year." I must add, that the evening alluded to was not passed *tête-à-tête*, but in a select company, of

which the present Lord Killmorey was one. "Molly
(says Dr. Johnson) was a beauty and a scholar, and
a wit and whig; and she talked all in praise of
liberty: and so I made this epigram upon her—
She was the lovelieſt creature I ever saw!!!

> *Liber ut esse velim, suasiſti pulchra Maria,*
> *Ut maneam liber—pulchra Maria, vale!"*

Will it do this way in English, Sir (said I)?

> Persuasions to freedom fall oddly from you;
> If freedom we seek—fair Maria, adieu!

"It will do well enough (replied he); but it is
translated by a lady, and the ladies never loved
M——y As——n." I asked him what his wife
thought of this attachment? "She was jealous to
be sure (said he), and teized me sometimes when
I would let her; and one day, as a fortune-telling
gipsey passed us when we were walking out in
company with two or three friends in the country,
she made the wench look at my hand, but soon
repented her curiosity; for (says the gipsey) Your
heart is divided, Sir, between a Betty and a Molly:
Betty loves you beſt, but you take moſt delight in
Molly's company: when I turned about to laugh,
I saw my wife was crying. Pretty charmer! she
had no reason!"

It was, I believe, long after the currents of life
had driven him to a great diſtance from this lady,
that he spent much of his time with Mrs. F—zh—-
b—t, of whom he always spoke with eſteem and

tenderness, and with a veneration very difficult to deserve. "That woman (said he) loved her husband as we hope and desire to be loved by our guardian angel. F—tzh—b—t was a gay good-humoured fellow, generous of his money and of his meat, and desirous of nothing but cheerful society among people distinguished in *some* way, in *any way* I think; for Rousseau and St. Austin would have been equally welcome to his table and to his kindness: the lady however was of another way of thinking; her first care was to preserve her husband's soul from corruption; her second, to keep his estate entire for their children: and I owed my good reception in the family to the idea she had entertained, that I was fit company for F—tzh—-b—t, whom I loved extremely. They dare not (said she) swear, and take other conversation-liberties before *you*." I asked if her husband returned her regard? "He felt her influence too powerfully (replied Mr. Johnson): no man will be fond of what forces him daily to feel himself inferior. She stood at the door of her Paradise in Derbyshire, like the angel with the flaming sword, to keep the devil at a distance. But she was not immortal, poor dear! she died, and her husband felt at once afflicted and released." I enquired if she was handsome? "She would have been handsome for a queen (replied the panegyrist); her beauty had more in it of majesty than of attraction, more of the dignity of virtue than the vivacity of wit." The

friend of this lady, Miss B—thby, succeeded her
in the management of Mr. F—tzh—b—t's family,
and in the esteem of Dr. Johnson; though he told
me she pushed her piety to bigotry, her devotion
to enthusiasm; that she somewhat disqualified herself for the duties of *this* life, by her perpetual
aspirations after the *next:* such was however the
purity of her mind, he said, and such the graces of
her manner, that Lord Lyttelton and he used to
strive for her preference with an emulation that
occasioned hourly disgust, and ended in lasting
animosity. "You may see (said he to me, when the
Poets Lives were printed) that dear B—thby is at
my heart still. She *would* delight in that fellow
Lyttelton's company though, for all that I could
do; and I cannot forgive even his memory the preference given by a mind like her's." I have heard
Baretti say, that when this lady died, Dr. Johnson
was almost distracted with his grief; and that the
friends about him had much ado to calm the
violence of his emotion. Dr. Taylor too related
once to Mr. Thrale and me, that when he lost his
wife, the negro Francis ran away, though in the
middle of the night, to Westminster, to fetch Dr.
Taylor to his master, who was all but wild with
excess of sorrow, and scarce knew him when he
arrived: after some minutes however, the doctor
proposed their going to prayers, as the only rational
method of calming the disorder this misfortune
had occasioned in both their spirits. Time, and

resignation to the will of God, cured every breach
in his heart before I made acquaintance with him,
though he always persisted in saying he never
rightly recovered the loss of his wife. It is in
allusion to her that he records the observation of
a female critic, as he calls her, in Gay's Life; and
the lady of great beauty and elegance, mentioned
in the criticisms upon Pope's epitaphs, was Miss
Molly Aston. The person spoken of in his strictures
upon Young's poetry, is the writer of these Anecdotes, to whom he likewise addressed the following
verses when he was in the Isle of Sky with Mr.
Boswell. The letters written in his journey, I used
to tell him, were better than the printed book; and
he was not displeased at my having taken the pains
to copy them all over. Here is the Latin ode:

> *Permeo terras, ubi nuda rupes*
> *Saxeas miscet nebulis ruinas,*
> *Torva ubi rident steriles coloni*
>   *Rura labores.*
>
> *Pervagor gentes, hominum ferorum*
> *Vita ubi nullo decorata cultu,*
> *Squallet informis, tigurique fumis*
>   *Fœda latescit.*
>
> *Inter erroris salebrosa longi,*
> *Inter ignotæ strepitus loquelæ,*
> *Quot modis mecum, quid agat requiro*
>   *Thralia dulcis?*
>
> *Seu viri curas pia nupta mulcet,*
> *Seu fovet mater sobolem benigna,*
> *Sive cum libris novitate pascit*
>   *Sedula mentem:*

Sit memor nostri, fideique merces,
Stet fides constans, meritoque blandum
Thraliæ discant resonare nomen
Littora Sciæ.

On another occasion I can boast verses from Dr. Johnson.—As I went into his room the morning of my birth-day once, and said to him, Nobody sends me any verses now, because I am five-and-thirty years old; and Stella was fed with them till forty-six, I remember. My being just recovered from illness and confinement will account for the manner in which he burst out suddenly, for so he did without the least previous hesitation whatsoever, and without having entertained the smallest intention towards it half a minute before:

> Oft in danger, yet alive,
> We are come to thirty-five;
> Long may better years arrive,
> Better years than thirty-five.
> Could philosophers contrive
> Life to stop at thirty-five,
> Time his hours should never drive
> O'er the bounds of thirty-five.
> High to soar, and deep to dive,
> Nature gives at thirty-five.
> Ladies, stock and tend your hive,
> Trifle not at thirty-five:
> For howe'er we boast and strive,
> Life declines from thirty-five:
> He that ever hopes to thrive
> Must begin by thirty-five;
> And all who wisely wish to wive
> Must look on Thrale at thirty-five.

"And now (said he, as I was writing them down), you may see what it is to come for poetry to a Dictionary-maker; you may observe that the rhymes run in alphabetical order exactly."——
And so they do.

Mr. Johnson did indeed possess an almost Tuscan power of improvisation: when he called to my daughter, who was consulting with a friend about a new gown and dressed hat she thought of wearing to an assembly, thus suddenly, while she hoped he was not listening to their conversation,

> Wear the gown, and wear the hat,
>   Snatch thy pleasures while they last;
> Hadst thou nine lives like a cat,
>   Soon those nine lives would be past.

It is impossible to deny to such little sallies the power of the Florentines, who do not permit their verses to be ever written down though they often deserve it, because, as they express it, *cosi se perderebbe la poca gloria.*

As for translations, we used to make him sometimes run off with one or two in a good humour. He was praising this song of Metastasio,

> *Deh, se piacermi vuoi,*
> *Lascia i sospetti tuoi,*
> *Non mi turbar conquesto*
> *Molesto dubitar:*
> *Chi ciecamente crede,*
> *Impegna a serbar fede;*
> *Chi sempre inganno aspetta,*
> *Alletta ad ingannar.*

"Should you like it in English (said he) thus?"

> Would you hope to gain my heart,
> Bid your teizing doubts depart;
> He who blindly trusts, will find
> Faith from every generous mind:
> He who still expects deceit,
> Only teaches how to cheat.

Mr. Baretti coaxed him likewise one day at Streatham out of a translation of Emirena's speech to the false courtier Aquileius, and it is probably printed before now, as I think two or three people took copies; but perhaps it has slipt their memories.

> *Ah! tu in corte invecchiasti, e giurerei*
> *Che fra i pochi non sei tenace ancora*
> *Dell' antica onestà: quando bisogna,*
> *Saprai sereno in volto*
> *Vezzeggiare un nemico; acciò vi cada,*
> *Aprirgli innanzi un precipizio, e poi*
> *Piangerne la caduta. Offrirti a tutti*
> *E non esser che tuo; di false lodi*
> *Vestir le accuse, ed aggravar le colpe*
> *Nel farne la difesa, ognor dal trono*
> *I buoni allontanar; d'ogni castigo*
> *Lasciar l'odio allo scettro, e d'ogni dono*
> *Il merito usurpar: tener nascosto*
> *Sotto un zelo apparente un empio fine,*
> *Ne fabbricar che sulle altrui rouine.*

Grown old in courts, thou art not surely one
Who keeps the rigid rules of ancient honour;
Well skill'd to sooth a foe with looks of kindness,
To sink the fatal precipice before him,
And then lament his fall with seeming friendship:

Open to all, true only to thyself,
Thou know'st those arts which blaſt with envious praise,
Which aggravate a fault with feign'd excuses,
And drive discountenanc'd virtue from the throne:
That leave the blame of rigour to the prince,
And of his every gift usurp the merit;
That hide in seeming zeal a wicked purpose,
And only build upon another's ruin.

These characters Dr. Johnson however did not delight in reading, or in hearing of: he always maintained that the world was not half as wicked as it was represented; and he might very well continue in that opinion, as he resolutely drove from him every ſtory that could make him change it; and when Mr. Bickerſtaff's flight confirmed the report of his guilt, and my husband said in answer to Johnson's aſtonishment, that he had long been a suspected man: "By those who look close to the ground, dirt will be seen, Sir (was the lofty reply): I hope I see things from a greater diſtance."

His desire to go abroad, particularly to see Italy, was very great; and he had a longing wish too to leave some Latin verses at the Grand Chartreux. He loved indeed the very act of travelling, and I cannot tell how far one might have taken him in a carriage before he would have wished for refreshment. He was therefore in some respects an admirable companion on the road, as he piqued himself upon feeling no inconvenience, and on despising no accommodations. On the other hand however, he expected no one else to feel any, and felt exceedingly inflamed with anger if any one complained of the rain, the sun, or the dust. "How (said he) do other people bear them?" As for general uneasiness, or complaints of long confinement in a carriage, he considered all lamentations on their account as proofs of an empty head, and a tongue desirous to talk without materials of conversation. "A mill that goes without grist (said he) is as good a companion as such creatures."

I pitied a friend before him, who had a whining wife that found every thing painful to her, and nothing pleasing—"He does not know that she whimpers (says Johnson); when a door has creaked for a fortnight together, you may observe—the master will scarcely give sixpence to get it oiled."

Of another lady, more insipid than offensive, I once heard him say, "She has some softness indeed, but so has a pillow." And when one observed in reply, that her husband's fidelity and attachment were exemplary, notwithstanding this low account at which her perfections were rated—"Why Sir (cries the Doctor), being married to those sleepy-souled women, is just like playing at cards for nothing: no passion is excited, and the time is filled up. I do not however envy a fellow one of those honey-suckle wives for my part, as they are but *creepers* at best, and commonly destroy the tree they so tenderly cling about."

For a lady of quality, since dead, who received us at her husband's seat in Wales with less attention

than he had long been accustomed to, he had a
rougher denunciation: "That woman (cries Johnson) is like sour small-beer, the beverage of her
table, and produce of the wretched country she
lives in: like that, she could never have been a good
thing, and even that bad thing is spoiled." This
was in the same vein of asperity, and I believe with
something like the same provocation, that he
observed of a Scotch lady, "that she resembled a
dead nettle; were she alive (said he), she would
sting."

Mr. Johnson's hatred of the Scotch is so well
known, and so many of his *bons mots* expressive of
that hatred have been already repeated in so many
books and pamphlets, that 'tis perhaps scarcely
worth while to write down the conversation between him and a friend of that nation who always
resides in London, and who at his return from the
Hebrides asked him, with a firm tone of voice,
What he thought of his country? "That it is a
very vile country to be sure, Sir," (returned for
answer Dr. Johnson.) Well, Sir! replies the other
somewhat mortified, God made it. "Certainly he
did (answers Mr. Johnson again); but we must
always remember that he made it for Scotchmen,
and comparisons are odious, Mr. S——; but God
made hell."

Dr. Johnson did not I think much delight in
that kind of conversation which consists in telling
stories: "every body (said he) tells stories of me,

and I tell stories of nobody. I do not recollect (added he), that I have ever told *you*, that have been always favourites, above three stories; but I hope I do not play the Old Fool, and force people to hear uninteresting narratives, only because I once was diverted with them myself." He was however an enemy to that sort of talk from the famous Mr. Foote, "whose happiness of manner in relating was such (he said) as subdued arrogance and roused stupidity: *His* stories were truly like those of Biron in Love's Labour Lost, so *very* attractive,

> That aged ears play'd truant with his tales,
> And younger hearings were quite ravish'd;
> So sweet and voluble was his discourse.

Of all conversers however (added he), the late Hawkins Browne was the most delightful with whom I ever was in company: his talk was at once so elegant, so apparently artless, so pure, and so pleasing, it seemed a perpetual stream of sentiment, enlivened by gaiety, and sparkling with images." When I asked Dr. Johnson, who was the *best* man he had ever known? "Psalmanazar," was the unexpected reply: he said, likewise, "that though a native of France, as his friend imagined, he possessed more of the English language than any one of the other foreigners who had separately fallen in his way. Though there was much esteem however, there was I believe but little confidence between them; they conversed merely about general topics, religion and learning, of which both were

undoubtedly ſtupendous examples; and, with regard to true Chriſtian perfeċtion, I have heard
Johnson say, "That George Psalmanazar's piety,
penitence, and virtue exceeded almoſt what we
read as wonderful even in the lives of saints."

I forget in what year it was that this extraordinary
person lived and died at a house in Old-ſtreet,
where Mr. Johnson was witness to his talents and
virtues, and to his final preference of the church
of England, after having ſtudied, disgraced, and
adorned so many modes of worship. The name he
went by, was not supposed by his friend to be that
of his family, but all enquiries were vain; his
reasons for concealing his original were peniten-
tiary; he deserved no other name than that of the
impoſtor, he said. That portion of the Universal
Hiſtory which was written by him, does not seem
to me to be composed with peculiar spirit, but all
traces of the wit and the wanderer were probably
worn out before he undertook the work.—His
pious and patient endurance of a tedious illness,
ending in an exemplary death, confirmed the ſtrong
impression his merit had made upon the mind of
Mr. Johnson. "It is so *very* difficult (said he,
always) for a sick man not to be a scoundrel. Oh!
set the pillows soft, here is Mr. Grumbler o'coming:
Ah! let no air in for the world, Mr. Grumbler will
be here presently."

This perpetual preference is so offensive where
the privileges of sickness are besides supported by

wealth, and nourished by dependence, that one
cannot much wonder that a rough mind is revolted
by them. It was however at once comical and
touchant (as the French call it), to observe Mr. Johnson so habitually watchful against this sort of behaviour, that he was often ready to suspect himself
of it; and when one asked him gently, how he
did?—"Ready to become a scoundrel, Madam
(would commonly be the answer): with a little
more spoiling you will, I think, make me a complete rascal."

His desire of doing good was not however
lessened by his aversion to a sick chamber: he
would have made an ill man well by any expence
or fatigue of his own, sooner than any of the
canters. Canter indeed was he none: he would
forget to ask people after the health of their nearest
relations, and say in excuse, "That he knew they
did not care: why should they? (says he;) every
one in this world has as much as they can do in
caring for themselves, and few have leisure really
to *think* of their neighbours distresses, however
they may delight their tongues with *talking* of
them."

The natural depravity of mankind and remains
of original sin were so fixed in Mr. Johnson's
opinion, that he was indeed a most acute observer
of their effects; and used to say sometimes, half in
jest half in earnest, that they were the remains of
his old tutor Mandeville's instructions. As a book

however, he took care always loudly to condemn the Fable of the Bees, but not without adding, "that it was the work of a thinking man."

I have in former days heard Dr. Collier of the Commons loudly condemned for uttering sentiments, which twenty years after I have heard as loudly applauded from the lips of Dr. Johnson, concerning the well-known writer of that celebrated work: but if people will live long enough in this capricious world, such inſtances of partiality will shock them less and less, by frequent repetition. Mr. Johnson knew mankind, and wished to mend them: he therefore, to the piety and pure religion, the untainted integrity, and scrupulous morals of my earlieſt and moſt disintereſted friend, judiciously contrived to join a cautious attention to the capacity of his hearers, and a prudent resolution not to lessen the influence of his learning and virtue, by casual freaks of humour, and irregular ſtarts of ill-managed merriment. He did not wish to confound, but to inform his auditors; and though he did not appear to solicit benevolence, he always wished to retain authority, and leave his company impressed with the idea, that it was his to teach in this world, and theirs to learn. What wonder then that all should receive with docility from Johnson those doctrines, which propagated by Collier they drove away from them with shouts! Dr. Johnson was not grave however because he knew not how to be merry. No man loved laughing better, and his vein of humour was rich, and apparently inexhaustible; though Dr. Goldsmith said once to him, We should change companions oftener, we exhaust one another, and shall soon be both of us worn out. Poor Goldsmith was to him indeed like the earthen pot to the iron one in Fontaine's fables; it had been better for *him* perhaps, that they had changed companions oftener; yet no experience of his antagonist's strength hindered him from continuing the contest. He used to remind me always of that verse in Berni,

Il pover uomo che non sen' èra accorto,
Andava combattendo—ed era morto.

Mr. Johnson made him a comical answer one day, when seeming to repine at the success of Beattie's Essay on Truth—"Here's such a stir (said he) about a fellow that has written one book, and I have written many." Ah, Doctor (says his friend), there go two-and-forty sixpences you know to one guinea.

They had spent an evening with Eaton Graham too, I remember hearing it was at some tavern; his heart was open, and he began inviting away; told what he could do to make his college agreeable, and begged the visit might not be delayed. Goldsmith thanked him, and proposed setting out with Mr. Johnson for Buckinghamshire in a fortnight; "Nay hold, Dr. *Minor* (says the other), I did not invite you."

Many such mortifications arose in the course of

their intimacy to be sure, but few more laughable
than when the newspapers had tacked them together
as the pedant and his flatterer in Love's Labour
loſt. Dr. Goldsmith came to his friend, fretting
and foaming, and vowing vengeance againſt the
printer, &c. till Mr. Johnson, tired of the buſtle,
and desirous to think of something else, cried out
at laſt, "Why, what would'ſt thou have, dear
Doctor! who the plague is hurt with all this nonsense? and how is a man the worse I wonder in his
health, purse, or character, for being called *Holofernes?*" I do not know (replies the other) how
you may relish being called Holofernes, but I do
not like at leaſt to play *Goodman Dull.*

Dr. Johnson was indeed famous for disregarding
public abuse. When the people criticised and
answered his pamphlets, papers, &c. "Why now,
these fellows are only advertising my book (he
would say); it is surely better a man should be
abused than forgotten." When Churchill nettled
him however, it is certain he felt the ſting, or that
poet's works would hardly have been left out of
the edition. Of that however I have no right
to decide; the booksellers perhaps did not put
Churchill on their liſt. I know Mr. Johnson was
exceedingly zealous to declare how very little he
had to do with the selection. Churchill's works too
might possibly be rejected by him upon a higher
principle; the higheſt indeed, if he was inspired
by the same laudable motive which made him

reject every authority for a word in his dictionary that could only be gleaned from writers dangerous to religion or morality—"I would not (said he) send people to look for words in a book, that by such a casual seizure of the mind might chance to mislead it for ever." In consequence of this delicacy, Mrs. Montague once observed, That were an angel to give the *imprimatur*, Dr. Johnson's works were among those very few which would not be lessened by a line. That such praise from such a lady should delight him, is not strange; insensibility in a case like that, must have been the result alone of arrogance acting on stupidity. Mr. Johnson had indeed no dislike to the commendations which he knew he deserved: "What signifies protesting so against flattery (would he cry)! when a person speaks well of one, it must be either true or false, you know; if true, let us rejoice in his good opinion; if he lies, it is a proof at least that he loves more to please me, than to sit silent when he need say nothing."

That natural roughness of his manner, so often mentioned, would, notwithstanding the regularity of his notions, burst through them all from time to time; and he once bade a very celebrated lady, who praised him with too much zeal perhaps, or perhaps too strong an emphasis (which always offended him), "consider what her flattery was worth before she choaked *him* with it." A few more winters passed in the talking world shewed him the value of that friend's commendations however; and he was very sorry for the disgusting speech he made her.

I used to think Mr. Johnson's determined preference of a cold monotonous talker over an emphatical and violent one, would make him quite a favourite among the men of *ton*, whose insensibility, or affectation of perpetual calmness, certainly did not give to him the offence it does to many. He loved "conversation without effort (he said);" and the encomiums I have heard him so often pronounce on the manners of Topham Beauclerc in society, constantly ended in that peculiar praise, that "it was without *effort*."

We were talking of Richardson who wrote Clarissa: "You think I love flattery (says Dr. Johnson), and so I do; but a little too much always disgusts me: that fellow Richardson, on the contrary, could not be contented to sail quietly down the stream of reputation, without longing to taste the froth from every stroke of the oar."

With regard to slight insults from newspaper abuse, I have already declared his notions: "They sting one (says he) but as a fly stings a horse; and the eagle will not catch flies." He once told me however, that Cummyns the famous Quaker, whose friendship he valued very highly, fell a sacrifice to their insults, having declared on his death-bed to Dr. Johnson, that the pain of an anonymous letter, written in some of the common prints of the day, fastened on his heart, and threw him into the slow fever of which he died.

Nor was Cummyns the only valuable member so lost to society: Hawkesworth, the pious, the virtuous, and the wise, for want of that fortitude which casts a shield before the merits of his friend, fell a lamented sacrifice to wanton malice and cruelty, I know not how provoked; but all in turn feel the lash of censure in a country where, as every baby is allowed to carry a whip, no person can escape except by chance. The unpublished crimes, unknown distresses, and even death itself, however, daily occurring in less liberal governments and less free nations, soon teach one to content one's self with such petty grievances, and make one acknowledge that the undistinguishing severity of newspaper abuse may in some measure diminish the diffusion of vice and folly in Great Britain, and while they fright delicate minds into forced refinements and affected insipidity, they are useful to the great causes of virtue in the soul, and liberty in the state; and though sensibility often sinks under the roughness of their prescriptions, it would be no good policy to take away their licence.

Knowing the state of Mr. Johnson's nerves, and how easily they were affected, I forbore reading in a new Magazine one day, the death of a Samuel Johnson who expired that month; but my companion snatching up the book, saw it himself, and contrary to my expectation—"Oh (said he)! I hope

Death will now be glutted with Sam. Johnsons, and let me alone for some time to come: I read of another namesake's departure laſt week."—Though Mr. Johnson was commonly affected even to agony at the thoughts of a friend's dying, he troubled himself very little with the complaints they might make to him about ill health. "Dear Doctor (said he one day to a common acquaintance, who lamented the tender ſtate of his *inside*), do not be like the spider, man; and spin conversation thus incessantly out of thy own bowels."—I told him of another friend who suffered grievously with the gout—"He will live a vaſt many years for all that (replied he), and then what signifies how much he suffers? but he will die at laſt, poor fellow, there's the misery; gout seldom takes the fort by a coup-de-main, but turning the siege into a blockade, obliges it to surrender at discretion."

A lady he thought well of, was disordered in her health—"What help has she called in (enquired Johnson)?" Dr. James, Sir; was the reply. "What is her disease?" Oh, nothing positive, rather a gradual and gentle decline. "She will die then, pretty dear (answered he)! When Death's pale horse runs away with persons on full speed, an active physician may possibly give them a turn; but if he carries them on an even slow pace, down hill too! no care nor skill can save them!"

When Garrick was on his laſt sick-bed, no arguments, or recitals of such facts as I had heard,

would persuade Mr. Johnson of his danger: he had
prepossessed himself with a notion, that to say a
man was sick, was very near wishing him so; and
few things offended him more, than prognosticating
even the death of an ordinary acquaintance. "Ay,
ay (said he), Swift knew the world pretty well,
when he said, that

> Some dire misfortune to portend,
> No enemy can match a friend."

The danger then of Mr. Garrick, or of Mr.
Thrale, whom he loved better, was an image which
no one durst present before his view; he always
persisted in the possibility and hope of their recovering from disorders from which no human creatures
by human means alone ever did recover. His distress for their loss was for that very reason poignant
to excess; but his fears of his own salvation were
excessive: his truly tolerant spirit, and Christian
charity, which *hopeth all things*, and *believeth all
things*, made him rely securely on the safety of his
friends, while his earnest aspiration after a blessed
immortality made him cautious of his own steps,
and timorous concerning their consequences. He
knew how much had been given, and filled his
mind with fancies of how much would be required,
till his impressed imagination was often disturbed
by them, and his health suffered from the sensibility
of his too tender conscience: a real Christian is *so*
apt to find his task above his power of performance!

Mr. Johnson did not however give into ridiculous refinements either of speculation or practice, or suffer himself to be deluded by specious appearances. "I have had dust thrown in my eyes too often (would he say), to be blinded so. Let us never confound matters of belief with matters of opinion." —Some one urged in his presence the preference of hope to possession; and as I remember, produced an Italian sonnet on the subject. "Let us not (cries Johnson) amuse ourselves with subtleties and sonnets, when speaking about hope, which is the follower of faith and the precursor of eternity; but if you only mean those air-built hopes which to-day excites and to-morrow will destroy, let us talk away, and remember that we only talk of the pleasures of hope; we feel those of possession, and no man in his senses would change the last for the first: such hope is a mere bubble, that by a gentle breath may be blown to what size you will almost, but a rough blast bursts it at once. Hope is an amusement rather than a good, and adapted to none but very tranquil minds." The truth is, Mr. Johnson hated what we call unprofitable chat; and to a gentleman who had disserted some time about the natural history of the mouse—"I wonder what such a one would have said (cried Johnson), if he had ever had the luck to see a *lion!*"

I well remember that at Brighthelmstone once, when he was not present, Mr. Beauclerc asserted that he was afraid of spirits; and I, who was secretly offended at the charge, asked him, the first opportunity I could find, What ground he had ever given to the world for such a report? "I can (replied he) recollect nothing nearer it, than my telling Dr. Lawrence many years ago, that a long time after my poor mother's death, I heard her voice call *Sam!*" What answer did the doctor make to your story, Sir, said I? "None in the world," (replied he;) and suddenly changed the conversation. Now as Mr. Johnson had a most unshaken faith, without any mixture of credulity, this story must either have been strictly true, or his persuasion of its truth the effect of disordered spirits. I relate the anecdote precisely as he told it me; but could not prevail on him to draw out the talk into length for further satisfaction of my curiosity.

As Johnson was the firmest of believers without being credulous, so he was the most charitable of mortals without being what we call an active friend. Admirable at giving counsel, no man saw his way so clearly; but he would not stir a finger for the assistance of those to whom he was willing enough to give advice: besides that, he had principles of laziness, and could be indolent by rule. To hinder your death, or procure you a dinner, I mean if really in want of one; his earnestness, his exertions could not be prevented, though health and purse and ease were all destroyed by their violence. If you wanted a slight favour, you must apply to people of other dispositions; for not a step would Johnson move to obtain a man a vote in a society, to repay a compliment which might be useful or pleasing, to write a letter of request, or to obtain a hundred pounds a year more for a friend, who perhaps had already two or three. No force could urge him to diligence, no importunity could conquer his resolution of standing still. "What good are we doing with all this ado (would he say)? dearest Lady, let's hear no more of it!" I have however more than once in my life forced him on such services, but with extreme difficulty.

We parted at his door one evening when I had teized him for many weeks to write a recommendatory letter of a little boy to his school-master; and after he had faithfully promised to do this prodigious feat before we met again—Do not forget dear Dick Sir, said I, as he went out of the coach: he turned back, stood still two minutes on the carriage-step—"When I have written my letter for Dick, I may hang myself, mayn't I?"—and turned away in a very ill humour indeed.

Though apt enough to take sudden likings or aversions to people he occasionally met, he would never hastily pronounce upon their character; and when seeing him justly delighted with Solander's conversation, I observed once that he was a man of great parts who talked from a full mind—"It may be so (said Mr. Johnson), but you cannot know it yet, nor I neither: the pump works well, to be sure! but how, I wonder, are we to decide in so very short an acquaintance, whether it is supplied by a spring or a reservoir?"—He always made a great difference in his esteem between talents and erudition; and when he saw a person eminent for literature, though wholly unconversable, it fretted him. "Teaching such tonies (said he to me one day), is like setting a lady's diamonds in lead, which only obscures the lustre of the stone, and makes the possessor ashamed on't." Useful and what we call every-day knowledge had the most of his just praise. "Let your boy learn arithmetic dear Madam," was his advice to the mother of a rich young heir: "he will not then be a prey to every rascal which this town swarms with: teach him the value of money, and how to reckon it; ignorance to a wealthy lad of one-and-twenty, is only so much fat to a sick sheep: it just serves to call the *rooks* about him."

> And all that prey in vice or folly
>   Joy to see their quarry fly;
> Here the gamester light and jolly,
>   There the lender grave and sly.

These improviso lines, making part of a long copy of verses which my regard for the youth on whose birth-day they were written obliges me to suppress lest they should give him pain, shew a mind of surprising activity and warmth; the more so as he was past seventy years of age when he composed them: but nothing more certainly offended Mr. Johnson, than the idea of a man's faculties (mental ones I mean) decaying by time; "It is not true, Sir (would he say); what a man could once do, he would always do, unless indeed by dint of vicious indolence, and compliance with the nephews and nieces who crowd round an old fellow, and help to tuck him in, till he, contented with the exchange of fame for ease, e'en resolves to let them set the pillows at his back, and gives no further proof of his exiſtence than juſt to suck the jelly that prolongs it."

For such a life or such a death Dr. Johnson was indeed never intended by Providence: his mind was like a warm climate, which brings every thing to perfection suddenly and vigorously, not like the alembicated productions of artificial fire, which always betray the difficulty of bringing them forth when their size is disproportionate to their flavour. *Je ferois un Roman tout comme un autre, mais la vie n'eſt point un Roman*, says a famous French writer; and this was so certainly the opinion of the Author of the Rambler, that all his conversation precepts tended towards the dispersion of romantic ideas, and were chiefly intended to promote the cultivation of

> That which before thee lies in daily life.
>
> MILTON.

And when he talked of authors, his praise went spontaneously to such passages as are sure in his own phrase to leave something behind them useful on common occasions, or observant of common manners. For example, it was not the two *laſt*, but the two *first*, volumes of Clarissa that he prized; "For give me a sick bed, and a dying lady (said he), and I'll be pathetic myself: but Richardson had picked the kernel of life (he said), while Fielding was contented with the husk." It was not King Lear cursing his daughters, or deprecating the storm, that I remember his commendations of; but Iago's ingenious malice, and subtle revenge; or prince Hal's gay compliance with the vices of Falstaff, whom he all along despised. Those plays had indeed no rivals in Johnson's favour: "No man but Shakespeare (he said) could have drawn Sir John."

His manner of criticising and commending Addison's prose, was the same in conversation as we read it in the printed strictures, and many of the expressions used have been heard to fall from him on common occasions. It was notwithstanding observable enough (or I fancied so), that he did never like, though he always thought fit to praise it; and his praises resembled those of a man who extols the superior elegance of high painted porcelain, while he himself always chuses to eat off *plate*. I told him so one day, and he neither denied it nor appeared displeased.

Of the pathetic in poetry he never liked to speak, and the only passage I ever heard him applaud as particularly tender in any common book, was Jane Shore's exclamation in the last act,

Forgive me! *but* forgive me!

It was not however from the want of a susceptible heart that he hated to cite tender expressions, for he was more strongly and more violently affected by the force of words representing ideas capable of affecting him at all, than any other man in the world I believe; and when he would try to repeat the celebrated *Prosa Ecclesiastica pro Mortuis*, as it is called, beginning *Dies iræ, Dies illa*, he could never pass the stanza ending thus, *Tantus labor non sit cassus*, without bursting into a flood of tears; which sensibility I used to quote against him when he would inveigh against devotional poetry, and protest that all religious verses were cold and feeble, and unworthy the subject, which ought to be treated with higher reverence, he said, than either poets or painters could presume to excite or bestow. Nor can any thing be a stronger proof of Dr. Johnson's piety than such an expression; for his idea of poetry was magnificent indeed, and very fully was he persuaded of its superiority over every other talent bestowed by heaven on man. His chapter upon that particular subject in his Rasselas, is really written from the fulness of his heart, and quite in his best manner I think. I am not so sure that this is the proper place to mention his writing that surprising little volume in a week or ten days time, in order to obtain money for his journey to Litchfield when his mother lay upon her last sickbed.

Promptitude of thought indeed, and quickness

of expression, were among the peculiar felicities of Johnson: his notions rose up like the dragon's teeth sowed by Cadmus all ready clothed, and in bright armour too, fit for immediate battle. He was therefore (as somebody is said to have expressed it) a tremendous converser, and few people ventured to try their skill against an antagonist with whom contention was so hopeless. One gentleman however, who dined at a nobleman's house in his company and that of Mr. Thrale, to whom I was obliged for the anecdote, was willing to enter the lists in defence of King William's character, and having opposed and contradicted Johnson two or three times petulantly enough; the master of the house began to feel uneasy, and expect disagreeable consequences: to avoid which he said, loud enough for the Doctor to hear, Our friend here has no meaning now in all this, except just to relate at club to-morrow how he teized Johnson at dinner to-day—this is all to do himself *honour.* No, upon my word, replied the other, I see no *honour* in it, whatever you may do. "Well, Sir! (returned Mr. Johnson sternly) if you do not *see* the *honour,* I am sure I *feel* the *disgrace.*"

A young fellow, less confident of his own abilities, lamenting one day that he had lost all his Greek—"I believe it happened at the same time, Sir (said Johnson), that I lost all my large estate in Yorkshire."

But however roughly he might be suddenly

provoked to treat a harmless exertion of vanity, he did not wish to inflict the pain he gave, and was sometimes very sorry when he perceived the people to smart more than they deserved. How harshly you treated that man to-day, said I once, who harangued us so about gardening—"I am sorry (said he) if I vexed the creature, for there certainly is no harm in a fellow's rattling a rattle-box, only don't let him think that he thunders."—The Lincolnshire lady who shewed him a grotto she had been making, came off no better as I remember: Would it not be a pretty cool habitation in summer? said she, Mr. Johnson! "I think it would, Madam (replied he),—for a toad."

All desire of distinction indeed had a sure enemy in Mr. Johnson. We met a friend driving six very small ponies, and stopt to admire them. "Why does nobody (said our doctor) begin the fashion of driving six spavined horses, all spavined of the same leg? it would have a mighty pretty effect, and produce the distinction of doing something worse than the common way."

When Mr. Johnson had a mind to compliment any one, he did it with more dignity to himself, and better effect upon the company, than any man. I can recollect but few instances indeed, though perhaps that may be more my fault than his. When Sir Joshua Reynolds left the room one day, he said, "There goes a man not to be spoiled by prosperity." And when Mrs. Montague shewed him some

China plates which had once belonged to Queen Elizabeth, he told her, "that they had no reason to be ashamed of their present possessor, who was so little inferior to the first." I likewise remember that he pronounced one day at my house a most lofty panegyric upon Jones the Orientalist, who seemed little pleased with the praise, for what cause I know not. He was not at all offended, when comparing all our acquaintance to some animal or other, we pitched upon the elephant for his resemblance, adding that the proboscis of that creature was like his mind most exactly, strong to buffet even the tyger, and pliable to pick up even the pin. The truth is, Mr. Johnson was often good-humouredly willing to join in childish amusements, and hated to be left out of any innocent merriment that was going forward. Mr. Murphy always said, he was incomparable at buffoonery; and I verily think, if he had had good eyes, and a form less inflexible, he would have made an admirable mimic.

He certainly rode on Mr. Thrale's old hunter with a good firmness, and though he would follow the hounds fifty miles an end sometimes, would never own himself either tired or amused. "I have now learned (said he), by hunting, to perceive, that it is no diversion at all, nor ever takes a man out of himself for a moment: the dogs have less sagacity than I could have prevailed on myself to suppose; and the gentlemen often call to me not to ride over them. It is very strange, and very melancholy, that the paucity of human pleasures should persuade us ever to call hunting one of them."—He was however proud to be amongſt the sportsmen; and I think no praise ever went so close to his heart, as when Mr. Hamilton called out one day upon Brighthelmſtone Downs, Why Johnson rides as well, for aught I see, as the moſt illiterate fellow in England.

Though Dr. Johnson owed his very life to air and exercise, given him when his organs of respiration could scarcely play, in the year 1766, yet he ever persiſted in the notion, that neither of them had any thing to do with health. "People live as long (said he) in Pepper-alley as on Salisbury-plain; and they live so much happier, that an inhabitant of the firſt would, if he turned cottager, ſtarve his underſtanding for want of conversation, and perish in a ſtate of mental inferiority."

Mr. Johnson indeed, as he was a very talking man himself, had an idea that nothing promoted happiness so much as conversation. A friend's erudition was commended one day as equally deep and ſtrong—"He will not talk Sir (was the reply), so his learning does no good, and his wit, if he has it, gives us no pleasure: out of all his boaſted ſtores I never heard him force but one word, and that word was *Richard*." With a contempt not inferior he received the praises of a pretty lady's face and behaviour: "She says nothing Sir (answers Johnson); a talking blackamoor were better than a white creature who adds nothing to life, and by sitting down before one thus desperately silent, takes away the confidence one should have in the company of her chair if she were once out of it."—No one was however less willing to begin any discourse than himself: his friend Mr. Thomas Tyers said, he was like the ghosts, who never speak till they are spoken to: and he liked the expression so well, that he often repeated it. He had indeed no necessity to lead the stream of chat to a favourite channel, that his fulness on the subject might be shewn more clearly, whatever was the topic; and he usually left the choice to others. His information best enlightened, his argument strengthened, and his wit made it ever remembered. Of him it might have been said, as he often delighted to say of Edmund Burke, "that you could not stand five minutes with that man beneath a shed while it rained, but you must be convinced you had been standing with the greatest man you had ever yet seen."

As we had been saying one day that no subject failed of receiving dignity from the manner in which Mr. Johnson treated it, a lady at my house said, she would make him talk about love; and took her measures accordingly, deriding the novels of the day because they treated about love. "It is not (replied our philosopher) because they treat, as you call it, about love, but because they treat of nothing, that they are despicable: we must not ridicule a passion which he who never felt never was happy, and he who laughs at never deserves to feel—a passion which has caused the change of empires, and the loss of worlds—a passion which has inspired heroism and subdued avarice." He thought he had already said too much. "A passion, in short (added he, with an altered tone), that consumes me away for my pretty Fanny here, and she is very cruel (speaking of another lady in the room)." He told us however in the course of the same chat, how his negro Francis had been eminent for his success among the girls. Seeing us all laugh, "I muſt have you know, ladies (said he), that Frank has carried the empire of Cupid further than moſt men. When I was in Lincolnshire so many years ago, he attended me thither; and when we returned home together, I found that a female haymaker had followed him to London for love." Francis was indeed no small favourite with his maſter, who retained however a prodigious influence over his moſt violent passions.

On the birth-day of our eldeſt daughter, and that of our friend Dr. Johnson, the 17th and 18th of September, we every year made up a little dance and supper, to divert our servants and their friends, putting the summer-house into their hands for the two evenings, to fill with acquaintance and merriment. Francis and his white wife were invited of course. She was eminently pretty, and he was jealous, as my maids told me. On the firſt of these days amusements (I know not what year) Frank took offence at some attentions paid his Desdemona, and walked away next morning to London in wrath. His master and I driving the same road an hour after, overtook him. "What is the matter, child (says Dr. Johnson), that you leave Streatham to-day? *Art sick?*" He is jealous (whispered I). "Are you jealous of your wife, you stupid blockhead (cries out his master in another tone)?" The fellow hesitated; and, *To be sure Sir, I don't quite approve Sir*, was the stammering reply. "Why, what do they *do* to her, man? do the footmen kiss her?" No Sir, no!—Kiss my *wife Sir!—I hope not Sir.* "Why, what *do* they do to her, my lad?" Why nothing Sir, I'm sure Sir. "Why then go back directly and dance you dog, do; and let's hear no more of such empty lamentations." I believe however that Francis was scarcely as much the object of Mr. Johnson's personal kindness, as the representative of Dr. Bathurst, for whose sake he would have loved any body, or any thing.

When he spoke of negroes, he always appeared to think them of a race naturally inferior, and made few exceptions in favour of his own; yet whenever disputes arose in his household among the many odd inhabitants of which it consisted, he always sided with Francis against the others, whom he suspected (not unjustly, I believe) of greater malignity. It seems at once vexatious and comical to reflect, that the dissentions those people chose to live constantly in, distressed and mortified him

exceedingly. He really was oftentimes afraid of
going home, because he was so sure to be met at
the door with numberless complaints; and he used
to lament pathetically to me, and to Mr. Saſtres
the Italian maſter, who was much his favourite,
that they made his life miserable from the impossibility he found of making theirs happy, when
every favour he beſtowed on one was wormwood
to the reſt. If, however, I ventured to blame their
ingratitude, and condemn their conduct, he would
inſtantly set about softening the one and juſtifying
the other; and finished commonly by telling me,
that I knew not how to make allowances for situations I never experienced.

> To thee no reason who know'ſt only good,
> But evil haſt not try'd.   Milton.

Dr. Johnson knew how to be merry with mean
people too, as well as to be sad with them; he
loved the lower ranks of humanity with a real
affection: and though his talents and learning kept
him always in the sphere of upper life, yet he
never loſt sight of the time when he and they
shared pain and pleasure in common. A borough
election once shewed me his toleration of boiſterous
mirth, and his content in the company of people
whom one would have thought at firſt sight little
calculated for his society. A rough fellow one day
on such an occasion, a hatter by trade, seeing Mr.
Johnson's beaver in a ſtate of decay, seized it
suddenly with one hand, and clapping him on the

back with the other; Ah, Master Johnson (says he),
this is no time to be thinking about *hats*. "No, no,
Sir (replies our Doctor in a cheerful tone), hats are
of no use now, as you say, except to throw up in
the air and huzza with;" accompanying his words
with the true election halloo.

But it was never against people of coarse life
that his contempt was expressed, while poverty of
sentiment in men who considered themselves to be
company for *the parlour*, as he called it, was what
he would not bear. A very ignorant young fellow,
who had plagued us all for nine or ten months,
died at last consumptive: "I think (said Mr. Johnson when he heard the news), I am afraid, I should
have been more concerned for the death of the *dog*;
but——(hesitating a while) I am not wrong now
in all this, for the dog acted up to his character on
every occasion that we know; but that dunce of
a fellow helped forward the general disgrace of
humanity." Why dear Sir (said I), how odd you
are! you have often said the lad was not capable
of receiving further instruction. "He was (replied
the Doctor) like a corked bottle, with a drop of
dirty water in it, to be sure; one might pump upon
it for ever without the smallest effect; but when
every method to open and clean it had been tried,
you would not have me grieve that the bottle was
broke at last."

This was the same youth who told us he had
been reading Lucius Florus; *Florus Delphini* was

the phrase; and my mother (said he) thought it had something to do with Delphos; but of that I know nothing. Who founded Rome then (enquired Mr. Thrale)? The lad replied, Romulus. And who succeeded Romulus (said I)? A long pause, and apparently distressful hesitation, followed the difficult question. "Why will you ask him in terms that he does not comprehend (said Mr. Johnson enraged)? You might as well bid him tell you who phlebotomised Romulus. This fellow's dulness is elastic (continued he), and all we do is but like kicking at a woolsack."

The pains he took however to obtain the young man more patient instructors, were many, and oftentimes repeated. He was put under the care of a clergyman in a distant province; and Mr. Johnson used both to write and talk to his friend concerning his education. It was on that occasion that I remember his saying, "A boy should never be sent to Eton or Westminster school before he is twelve years old at least; for if in his years of babyhood he 'scapes that general and transcendent knowledge without which life is perpetually put to a stand, he will never get it at a public school, where if he does not learn Latin and Greek, he learns nothing." Mr. Johnson often said, "that there was too much stress laid upon literature as indispensably necessary: there is surely no need that every body should be a scholar, no call that every one should square the circle. Our manner of teaching (said he) cramps and warps many a mind, which if left more at liberty would have been respectable in some way, though perhaps not in that. We lop our trees, and prune them, and pinch them about (he would say), and nail them tight up to the wall, while a good standard is at last the only thing for bearing healthy fruit, though it commonly begins later. Let the people learn necessary knowledge; let them learn to count their fingers, and to count their money, before they are caring for the classics; for (says Mr. Johnson) though I do not quite agree with the proverb, that *Nullum numen abest si sit prudentia*, yet we may very well say, that *Nullum numen adest—ni sit prudentia.*"

We had been visiting at a lady's house, whom as we returned some of the company ridiculed for her ignorance: "She is not ignorant (said he), I believe, of any thing she has been taught, or of any thing she is desirous to know; and I suppose if one wanted a little *run tea*, she might be a proper person enough to apply to."

When I relate these various instances of contemptuous behaviour shewn to a variety of people, I am aware that those who till now have heard little of Mr. Johnson will here cry out against his pride and his severity; yet I have been as careful as I could to tell them, that all he did was gentle, if all he said was rough. Had I given anecdotes of his actions instead of his words, we should I am sure have had nothing on record but acts of virtue

differently modified, as different occasions called
that virtue forth: and among all the nine biographical essays or performances which I have
heard will at laſt be written about dear Dr. Johnson, no mean or wretched, no wicked or even
slightly culpable aċtion will I truſt be found, to
produce and put in the scale againſt a life of seventy
years, spent in the uniform praċtice of every moral
excellence and every Chriſtian perfeċtion, save
humility alone, says a critic, but that I think *muſt*
be excepted. He was not however wanting even
in that to a degree seldom attained by man, when
the duties of piety or charity called it forth.

Lowly towards God, and docile towards the
church; implicit in his belief of the gospel, and
ever respeċtful towards the people appointed to
preach it; tender of the unhappy, and affeċtionate
to the poor, let no one haſtily condemn as proud,
a charaċter which may perhaps somewhat juſtly be
censured as arrogant. It muſt however be remembered again, that even this arrogance was never
shewn without some intention, immediate or remote, of mending some fault or conveying some
inſtruċtion. Had I meant to make a panegyric on
Mr. Johnson's well-known excellencies, I should
have told his deeds only, not his words—sincerely
proteſting, that as I never saw him once do a wrong
thing, so we had accuſtomed ourselves to look
upon him almoſt as an excepted being; and I
should as much have expeċted injuſtice from

Socrates or impiety from Paschal, as the slightest
deviation from truth and goodness in any trans-
action one might be engaged in with Samuel Johnson. His attention to veracity was without equal
or example: and when I mentioned Clarissa as a
perfect character; "On the contrary (said he), you
may observe there is always something which she
prefers to truth. Fielding's Amelia was the most
pleasing heroine of all the romances (he said); but
that vile broken nose never cured, ruined the sale
of perhaps the only book, which being printed off
betimes one morning, a new edition was called for
before night."

Mr. Johnson's knowledge of literary history
was extensive and surprising: he knew every ad-
venture of every book you could name almost, and
was exceedingly pleased with the opportunity which
writing the Poets Lives gave him to display it. He
loved to be set at work, and was sorry when he
came to the end of the business he was about. I do
not feel so myself with regard to these sheets: a
fever which has preyed on me while I wrote them
over for the press, will perhaps lessen my power
of doing well the first, and probably the last work
I should ever have thought of presenting to the
Public. I could doubtless wish so to conclude it,
as at least to shew my zeal for my friend, whose
life, as I once had the honour and happiness of
being useful to, I should wish to record a few
particular traits of, that those who read should

emulate his goodness; but seeing the necessity of making even virtue and learning such as *his* agreeable, that all should be warned against such coarseness of manners, as drove even from *him* those who loved, honoured, and esteemed him. His wife's daughter, Mrs. Lucy Porter of Litchfield, whose veneration for his person and character has ever been the greatest possible, being opposed one day in conversation by a clergyman who came often to her house, and feeling somewhat offended, cried out suddenly, Why, Mr. Pearson, said she, you are just like Dr. Johnson, I think: I do not mean that you are a man of the greatest capacity in all the world like Dr. Johnson, but that you contradict one every word one speaks, just like him.

Mr. Johnson told me the story: he was present at the giving of the reproof. It was however observable that with all his odd severity, he could not keep even indifferent people from teizing him with unaccountable confessions of silly conduct which one would think they would scarcely have had inclination to reveal even to their tenderest and most intimate companions; and it was from these unaccountable volunteers in sincerity that he learned to warn the world against follies little known, and seldom thought on by other moralists.

Much of his eloquence, and much of his logic have I heard him use to prevent men from making vows on trivial occasions; and when he saw a person oddly perplexed about a slight difficulty,

"Let the man alone (he would say), and torment him no more about it; there is a vow in the case, I am convinced; but is it not very strange that people should be neither afraid nor ashamed of bringing in God Almighty thus at every turn between themselves and their dinner?" When I asked what ground he had for such imaginations, he informed me, "That a young lady once told him in confidence, that she could never persuade herself to be dressed against the bell rung for dinner, till she had made a vow to heaven that she would never more be absent from the family meals."

The strangest applications in the world were certainly made from time to time towards Mr. Johnson, who by that means had an inexhaustible fund of anecdote, and could, if he pleased, tell the most astonishing stories of human folly and human weakness that ever were confided to any man not a confessor by profession.

One day when he was in a humour to record some of them, he told us the following tale: "A person (said he) had for these last five weeks often called at my door, but would not leave his name, or other message; but that he wished to speak with me. At last we met, and he told me that he was oppressed by scruples of conscience: I blamed him gently for not applying, as the rules of our church direct, to his parish priest or other discreet clergyman; when, after some compliments on his part, he told me, that he was clerk to a very eminent

trader, at whose warehouses much business consisted in packing goods in order to go abroad: that
he was often tempted to take paper and packthread
enough for his own use, and that he had indeed
done so so often, that he could recollect no time
when he ever had bought any for himself.—But
probably (said I), your master was wholly indifferent with regard to such trivial emoluments;
you had better ask for it at once, and so take your
trifles with consent.—Oh, Sir! replies the visitor,
my master bid me have as much as I pleased, and
was half angry when I talked to him about it.—
Then pray Sir (said I), teize me no more about such
airy nothings;—and was going on to be very angry,
when I recollected that the fellow might be mad
perhaps; so I asked him, When he left the counting-
house of an evening?—At seven o'clock, Sir.—
And when do you go to-bed, Sir?—At twelve
o'clock.—Then (replied I) I have at least learned
thus much by my new acquaintance;—that five
hours of the four-and-twenty unemployed are
enough for a man to go mad in; so I would advise
you Sir, to study algebra, if you are not an adept
already in it: your head would get less *muddy*, and
you will leave off tormenting your neighbours
about paper and packthread, while we all live
together in a world that is bursting with sin and
sorrow. It is perhaps needless to add, that this
visitor came no more."

Mr. Johnson had indeed a real abhorrence of a

person that had ever before him treated a little
thing like a great one: and he quoted this scrupulous gentleman with his packthread very often, in
ridicule of a friend who, looking out on Streatham
Common from our windows one day, lamented the
enormous wickedness of the times, because some
bird-catchers were busy there one fine Sunday
morning. "While half the Chriſtian world is permitted (said he) to dance and sing, and celebrate
Sunday as a day of feſtivity, how comes your
puritanical spirit so offended with frivolous and
empty deviations from exaćtness. Whoever loads
life with unnecessary scruples, Sir (continued he),
provokes the attention of others on his condućt,
and incurs the censure of singularity without reap-
ing the reward of superior virtue."

I muſt not, among the anecdotes of Dr. Johnson's life, omit to relate a thing that happened to
him one day, which he told me of himself. As he
was walking along the Strand a gentleman ſtepped
out of some neighbouring tavern, with his napkin
in his hand and no hat, and ſtopping him as civilly
as he could—I beg your pardon, Sir; but you are
Dr. Johnson, I believe. "Yes, Sir." We have a
wager depending on your reply: Pray, Sir, is it
irrèparable or irrepàirable that one should say?
"The *laſt* I think, Sir (answered Dr. Johnson), for
the adjećtive ought to follow the verb; but you
had better consult my dićtionary than me, for that
was the result of more thought than you will now

give me time for." No, no, replied the gentleman
gaily, the book I have no certainty at all of; but
here is the *author*, to whom I referred: Is he not,
Sir? to a friend with him: I have won my twenty
guineas quite fairly, and am much obliged to you,
Sir; so shaking Mr. Johnson kindly by the hand,
he went back to finish his dinner or desert.

Another ſtrange thing he told me once which
there was no danger of forgetting: how a young
gentleman called on him one morning, and told
him that his father having, juſt before his death,
dropped suddenly into the enjoyment of an ample
fortune, he, the son, was willing to qualify himself
for genteel society by adding some literature to his
other endowments, and wished to be put in an easy
way of obtaining it. Johnson recommended the
university; "for you read Latin, Sir, with *facility*."
I read it a little to be sure, Sir. "But do you read
it *with facility*, I say?" Upon my word, Sir, I do
not very well know, but I rather believe not. Mr.
Johnson now began to recommend other branches
of science, when he found languages at such an
immeasurable diſtance, and advising him to ſtudy
natural hiſtory, there arose some talk about animals,
and their divisions into oviparous and viviparous;
And the cat here, Sir, said the youth who wished
for inſtruction, pray in which class is she? Our
doctor's patience and desire of doing good began
now to give way to the natural roughness of his
temper. "You would do well (said he) to look for

some person to be always about you, Sir, who is capable of explaining such matters, and not come to us (there were some literary friends present as I recollect) to know whether the cat lays eggs or not: get a discreet man to keep you company, there are so many who would be glad of your table and fifty pounds a year." The young gentleman retired, and in less than a week informed his friends that he had fixed on a preceptor to whom no objections could be made; but when he named as such one of the most distinguished characters in our age or nation, Mr. Johnson fairly gave himself up to an honest burst of laughter; and seeing this youth at such a surprising distance from common knowledge of the world, or of any thing in it, desired to see his visitor no more.

He had not much better luck with two boys that he used to tell of, to whom he had taught the classics, "so that (he said) they were no incompetent or mean scholars:" it was necessary however that something more familiar should be known, and he bid them read the history of England. After a few months had elapsed he asked them, "If they could recollect who first destroyed the monasteries in our island?" One modestly replied, that he did not know; the other said, *Jesus Christ.*

Of the truth of stories which ran currently about the town concerning Dr. Johnson, it was impossible to be certain, unless one asked him himself; and what he told, or suffered to be told before his face

without contradicting, has every possible mark I
think of real and genuine authenticity. I made one
day very minute enquiries about the tale of his
knocking down the famous Tom Osborne with his
own Dictionary in the man's own house. And how
was that affair, in earnest? do tell me, Mr. Johnson? "There is nothing to tell, dearest Lady, but
that he was insolent and I beat him, and that he
was a blockhead and told of it, which I should
never have done; so the blows have been multi-
plying, and the wonder thickening for all these
years, as Thomas was never a favourite with the
Public. I have beat many a fellow, but the rest
had the wit to hold their tongues."

I have heard Mr. Murphy relate a very singular
story, while he was present, greatly to the credit of
his uncommon skill and knowledge of life and
manners: When first the Ramblers came out in
separate numbers, as they were the objects of
attention to multitudes of people, they happened,
as it seems, particularly to attract the notice of a
society who met every Saturday evening during
the summer at Rumford in Essex, and were known
by the name of The Bowling-green Club. These
men seeing one day the character of Leviculus the
fortune-hunter, or Tetrica the old maid: another
day some account of a person who spent his life
in hoping for a legacy, or of him who is always
prying into other folks affairs, began sure enough
to think they were betrayed; and that some of the

coterie sate down to divert himself by giving to the
Public the portrait of all the rest. Filled with
wrath against the traitor of Rumford, one of them
resolved to write to the printer and enquire the
author's name; Samuel Johnson, was the reply.
No more was necessary; Samuel Johnson was the
name of the curate, and soon did each begin to
load him with reproaches for turning his friends
into ridicule in a manner so cruel and unprovoked.
In vain did the guiltless curate protest his inno-
cence; one was sure that Aliger meant Mr. Twigg,
and that Cupidus was but another name for neighbour Baggs: till the poor parson, unable to contend
any longer, rode to London, and brought them full
satisfaction concerning the writer, who from his
own knowledge of general manners, quickened by
a vigorous and warm imagination, had happily
delineated, though unknown to himself, the members of the Bowling-green Club.

Mr. Murphy likewise used to tell before Dr.
Johnson, of the first time *they* met, and the occasion
of their meeting, which he related thus: That being
in those days engaged in a periodical paper, he
found himself at a friend's house out of town; and
not being disposed to lose pleasure for the sake of
business, wished rather to content his bookseller
by sending some unstudied essay to London by
the servant, than deny himself the company of his
acquaintance, and drive away to his chambers for
the purpose of writing something more correct.

He therefore took up a French *Journal Literaire* that lay about the room, and translating something he liked from it, sent it away without further examination. Time however discovered that he had translated from the French a Rambler of Johnson's which had been but a month before taken from the English; and thinking it right to make him his personal excuses, he went next day, and found our friend all covered with soot like a chimney-sweeper, in a little room, with an intolerable heat and strange smell, as if he had been acting Lungs in the Alchymist, making *æther*. "Come, come (says Dr. Johnson), dear Mur, the story is black enough now; and it was a very happy day for me that brought you first to my house, and a very happy mistake about the Ramblers."

Dr. Johnson was always exceeding fond of chemistry; and we made up a sort of laboratory at Streatham one summer, and diverted ourselves with drawing essences and colouring liquors. But the danger Mr. Thrale found his friend in one day when I was driven to London, and he had got the children and servants round him to see some experiments performed, put an end to all our entertainment; so well was the master of the house persuaded, that his short sight would have been his destruction in a moment, by bringing him close to a fierce and violent flame. Indeed it was a perpetual miracle that he did not set himself on fire reading a-bed, as was his constant custom, when exceedingly unable even to keep clear of mischief with our best help; and accordingly the fore-top of all his wigs were burned by the candle down to the very net-work. Mr. Thrale's valet-de-chambre, for that reason, kept one always in his own hands, with which he met him at the parlour-door when the bell had called him down to dinner, and as he went up stairs to sleep in the afternoon, the same man constantly followed him with another.

Future experiments in chemistry however were too dangerous, and Mr. Thrale insisted that we should do no more towards finding the philosophers stone.

Mr. Johnson's amusements were thus reduced to the pleasures of conversation merely: and what wonder that he should have an avidity for the sole delight he was able to enjoy? No man conversed so well as he on every subject; no man so acutely discerned the reason of every fact, the motive of every action, the end of every design. He was indeed often pained by the ignorance or causeless wonder of those who knew less than himself, though he seldom drove them away with apparent scorn, unless he thought they added presumption to stupidity: And it was impossible not to laugh at the patience he shewed, when a Welch parson of mean abilities, though a good heart, struck with reverence at the sight of Dr. Johnson, whom he had heard of as the greatest man living, could not find any words to answer his inquiries concerning a motto round somebody's arms which adorned a tomb-stone in Ruabon church-yard. If I remember right the words were,

> *Heb Dw, Heb Dym,*
> *Dw o' diggon.*

And though of no very difficult construction, the gentleman seemed wholly confounded, and unable to explain them; till Mr. Johnson having picked out the meaning by little and little, said to the man, "*Heb* is a preposition, I believe Sir, is it not?" My countryman recovering some spirits upon the sudden question, cried out, So I humbly presume Sir, very comically.

Stories of humour do not tell well in books; and what made impression on the friends who heard a jest, will seldom much delight the distant acquaintance or sullen critic who reads it. The cork model of Paris is not more despicable as a resemblance of a great city, than this book, *levior cortice*, as a specimen of Johnson's character. Yet every body naturally likes to gather little specimens of the rarities found in a great country; and could I carry home from Italy square pieces of all the curious marbles which are the just glory of this surprising part of the world, I could scarcely contrive perhaps to arrange them so meanly as not to gain some attention from the respect due to the places they once belonged to.——Such a piece of motley Mosaic work will these Anecdotes inevitably make: but let the reader remember that he was promised nothing better, and so be as contented as he can.

An Irish trader at our house one day heard Dr. Johnson launch out into very great and greatly deserved praises of Mr. Edmund Burke: delighted to find his countryman ſtood so high in the opinion of a man he had been told so much of, Sir (said he), give *me* leave to tell something of Mr. Burke now. We were all silent, and the honeſt Hibernian began to relate how Mr. Burke went to see the collieries in a diſtant province; and he would go down into the bowels of the earth (in a bag), and he would examine every thing: he went in a bag Sir, and ventured his health and his life for knowledge; but he took care of his clothes, that they should not be spoiled, for he went down in a bag. "Well Sir (says Mr. Johnson good-humouredly), if our friend Mund should die in any of these hazardous exploits, you and I would write his life and panegyric together; and your chapter of it should be entitled thus: *Burke in a Bag.*"

He had always a very great personal regard and particular affeƈtion for Mr. Edmund Burke, as well as an eſteem difficult for me to repeat, though for him only easy to express. And when at the end of the year 1774 the general eleƈtion called us all different ways, and broke up the delightful society in which we had spent some time at Beconsfield, Dr. Johnson shook the hospitable maſter of the house kindly by the hand, and said, "Farewell my dear Sir, and remember that I wish you all the success which ought to be wished you, which can possibly be wished you indeed—*by an honeſt man.*"

I muſt here take leave to observe, that in giving little memoirs of Mr. Johnson's behaviour and conversation, such as I saw and heard it, my book lies under manifeſt disadvantages, compared with theirs, who having seen him in various situations, and observed his conduct in numberless cases, are able to throw ſtronger and more brilliant lights upon his character. Virtues are like shrubs, which yield their sweets in different manners according to the circumſtances which surround them: and while generosity of soul scatters its fragrance like the honeysuckle, and delights the senses of many occasional passengers, who feel the pleasure, and half wonder how the breeze has blown it from so far, the more sullen but not less valuable myrtle waits like fortitude to discover its excellence, till the hand arrives that will *crush* it, and force out that perfume whose durability well compensates the difficulty of production.

I saw Mr. Johnson in none but a tranquil uniform ſtate, passing the evening of his life among friends, who loved, honoured, and admired him: I saw none of the things he did, except such acts of charity as have been often mentioned in this book, and such writings as are universally known. What he said is all I can relate; and from what he said, those who think it worth while to read these

Anecdotes, muſt be contented to gather his cha-
raЄter. Mine is a mere *candle-light* piЄture of his
latter days, where every thing falls in dark shadow
except the face, the index of the mind; but even
that is seen unfavourably, and with a paleness
beyond what nature gave it.

When I have told how many follies Dr. Johnson
knew of others, I muſt not omit to mention with
how much fidelity he would always have kept them
concealed, could they of whom he knew the absur-
dities have been contented, in the common phrase,
to keep their own counsel. But returning home one
day from dining at the chaplain's table, he told
me, that Dr. Goldsmith had given a very comical
and unnecessarily exaЄt recital there, of his own
feelings when his play was hissed; telling the company how he went indeed to the Literary Club at
night, and chatted gaily among his friends, as if
nothing had happened amiss; that to impress them
ſtill more forcibly with an idea of his magnanimity,
he even sung his favourite song about an old woman
tossed in a blanket seventeen times as high as the
moon; but all this while I was suffering horrid
tortures (said he), and verily believe that if I had
put a bit into my mouth it would have ſtrangled
me on the spot, I was so excessively ill; but I made
more noise than usual to cover all that, and so they
never perceived my not eating, nor I believe at all
imaged to themselves the anguish of my heart:
but when all were gone except Johnson here, I

burst out a-crying, and even swore by —— that I would never write again. "All which, Doctor (says Mr. Johnson, amazed at his odd frankness), I thought had been a secret between you and me! and I am sure I would not have said any thing about it for the world. Now see (repeated he when he told the story) what a figure a man makes who thus unaccountably chuses to be the frigid narrator of his own disgrace. *Il volto sciolto, ed i pensieri stretti*, was a proverb made on purpose for such mortals, to keep people, if possible, from being thus the heralds of their own shame: for what compassion can they gain by such silly narratives? No man should be expected to sympathise with the sorrows of vanity. If then you are mortified by any ill usage, whether real or supposed, keep at least the account of such mortifications to yourself, and forbear to proclaim how meanly you are thought on by others, unless you desire to be meanly thought of by all."

The little history of another friend's superfluous ingenuity will contribute to introduce a similar remark. He had a daughter of about fourteen years old, as I remember, fat and clumsy: and though the father adored, and desired others to adore her, yet being aware perhaps that she was not what the French call *paitrie des graces*, and thinking I suppose that the old maxim, of beginning to laugh at yourself first where you have any thing ridiculous about you, was a good one, he

comically enough called his girl *Trundle* when he
spoke of her; and many who bore neither of them
any ill-will felt disposed to laugh at the happiness
of the appellation. "See now (says Dr. Johnson)
what haste people are in to be hooted. Nobody
ever thought of this fellow nor of his daughter,
could he but have been quiet himself, and forborne
to call the eyes of the world on his dowdy and her
deformity. But it teaches one to see at least, that
if nobody else will nickname one's children, the
parents will e'en do it themselves."

All this held true in matters to Mr. Johnson of
more serious consequence. When Sir Joshua Reynolds had painted his portrait looking into the slit
of his pen, and holding it almost close to his eye,
as was his general custom, he felt displeased, and
told me "he would not be known by posterity for
his *defects* only, let Sir Joshua do his worst." I said
in reply, that Reynolds had no such difficulties
about himself, and that he might observe the
picture which hung up in the room where we were
talking, represented Sir Joshua holding his ear in
his hand to catch the sound. "He may paint himself as deaf if he chuses (replied Johnson); but I
will not be *blinking Sam*."

It is chiefly for the sake of evincing the regularity
and steadiness of Mr. Johnson's mind that I have
given these trifling memoirs, to shew that his soul
was not different from that of another person, but,
as it was, greater; and to give those who did not

know him a just idea of his acquiescence in what we call vulgar prejudices, and of his extreme distance from those notions which the world has agreed, I know not very well why, to call romantic. It is indeed observable in his preface to Shakespeare, that while other critics expatiate on the creative powers and vivid imagination of that matchless poet, Dr. Johnson commends him for giving so just a representation of human manners, "that from his scenes a hermit might estimate the value of society, and a confessor predict the progress of the passions." I have not the book with me here, but am pretty sure that such is his expression.

The general and constant advice he gave too, when consulted about the choice of a wife, a profession, or whatever influences a man's particular and immediate happiness, was always to reject no positive good from fears of its contrary consequences. "Do not (said he) forbear to marry a beautiful woman if you can find such, out of a fancy that she will be less constant than an ugly one; or condemn yourself to the society of coarseness and vulgarity for fear of the expences or other dangers of elegance and personal charms, which have been always acknowledged as a positive good, and for the want of which there should be always given some weighty compensation. I have however (continued Mr. Johnson) seen some prudent fellows who forbore to connect themselves with beauty lest coquetry should be near, and with wit or birth left insolence should lurk behind them, till they have been forced by their discretion to linger life away in tasteless stupidity, and chuse to count the moments by remembrance of pain instead of enjoyment of pleasure."

When professions were talked of, "Scorn (said Mr. Johnson) to put your behaviour under the dominion of canters; never think it clever to call physic a mean study, or law a dry one; or ask a baby of seven years old which way *his genius* leads him, when we all know that a boy of seven years old has no *genius* for any thing except a peg-top and an apple-pye; but fix on some business where much money may be got and little virtue risqued: follow that business steadily, and do not live as Roger Ascham says the wits do, *Men know not how*; *and at last die obscurely, men mark not where.*"

Dr. Johnson had indeed a veneration for the voice of mankind beyond what most people will own; and as he liberally confessed that all his own disappointments proceeded from himself, he hated to hear others complain of general injustice. I remember when lamentation was made of the neglect shewed to Jeremiah Markland, a great philologist as some one ventured to call him—"He is a scholar undoubtedly Sir (replied Dr. Johnson), but remember that he would run from the world, and that it is not the world's business to run after him. I hate a fellow whom pride, or cowardice, or laziness drives into a corner, and who does nothing when he is there but sit and *growl*; let him come out as I do, and *bark*. The world (added he) is chiefly unjuſt and ungenerous in this, that all are ready to encourage a man who once talks of leaving it, and few things do really provoke me more, than to hear people prate of retirement, when they have neither skill to discern their own motives, or penetration to eſtimate the consequences: but while a fellow is active to gain either power or wealth (continued he), every body produces some hindrance to his advancement, some sage remark, or some unfavourable prediction; but let him once say slightly, I have had enough of this troublesome buſtling world, 'tis time to leave it now: Ah, dear Sir! cries the firſt old acquaintance he meets, I am glad to find you in this happy disposition: yes, dear friend! *do* retire and think of nothing but your own ease: there's Mr. William will find it a pleasure to settle all your accounts and relieve you from the fatigue; Miss Dolly makes the charmingeſt chicken broth in the world, and the cheesecakes we eat of her's once, how good they were: I will be coming every two or three days myself to chat with you in a quiet way; *so snug!* and tell you how matters go upon 'Change, or in the House, or according to the blockhead's firſt pursuits, whether lucrative or politic, which thus he leaves; and lays himself down a voluntary prey to his own sensuality and sloth, while the ambition and avarice of the nephews and nieces, with their rascally adherents and coadjutors, reap the advantage, while they fatten their fool."

As the votaries of retirement had little of Mr. Johnson's applause, unless that he knew that the motives were merely devotional, and unless he was convinced that their rituals were accompanied by a mortified state of the body, the sole proof of their sincerity which he would admit, as a compensation for such fatigue as a worldly life of care and activity requires; so of the various states and conditions of humanity, he despised none more I think than the man who marries for a maintenance: and of a friend who made his alliance on no higher principles, he said once, "Now has that fellow (it was a nobleman of whom we were speaking) at length obtained a certainty of three meals a day, and for that certainty, like his brother dog in the fable, he will get his neck galled for life with a collar."

That poverty was an evil to be avoided by all honest means however, no man was more ready to avow: concealed poverty particularly, which he said was the general corrosive that destroyed the peace of almost every family; to which no evening perhaps ever returned without some new project for hiding the sorrows and dangers of the next day. "Want of money (says Dr. Johnson) is sometimes concealed under pretended avarice, and sly hints of aversion to part with it; sometimes under stormy anger, and affectation of boundless rage; but oftener still under a shew of thoughtless extravagance and gay neglect—while to a penetrating eye, none of these wretched veils suffice to keep the cruel truth from being seen. Poverty is *hic et ubique* (says he), and if you do shut the jade out of the door, she will always contrive in some manner to poke her pale lean face in at the window."

I have mentioned before, that old age had very little of Mr. Johnson's reverence: "a man commonly grew wickeder as he grew older (he said), at least he but changed the vices of youth; headstrong passion and wild temerity, for treacherous caution, and desire to circumvent. I am always (said he) on the young people's side, when there is a dispute between them and the old ones: for you have at least a chance for virtue till age has withered its very root." While we were talking, my mother's spaniel, whom he never loved, stole our toast and butter; Fye Belle! said I, you used to be upon honour: "Yes Madam (replies Johnson), *but Belle grows old.*" His reason for hating the dog was, "because she was a professed favourite (he said), and because her Lady ordered her from time to time to be washed and combed: a foolish trick (said he) and an assumption of superiority that every one's nature revolts at; so because one must not wish ill to the Lady in such cases (continued he), one curses the cur." The truth is, Belle was not well behaved, and being a large spaniel, was troublesome enough at dinner with frequent solicitations to be fed. "This animal (said Dr. Johnson one day) would have been of extraordinary merit and value in the State of Lycurgus; for she condemns one to the exertion of perpetual vigilance."

He had indeed that strong aversion felt by all the lower ranks of people towards four-footed companions very completely, notwithstanding he had for many years a cat which he called Hodge, that kept always in his room at Fleet-Street; but so exact was he not to offend the human species by superfluous attention to brutes, that when the creature was grown sick and old, and could eat nothing but oysters, Mr. Johnson always went out himself to buy Hodge's dinner, that Francis the Black's delicacy might not be hurt, at seeing himself employed for the convenience of a quadruped.

No one was indeed so attentive not to offend in all such sort of things as Dr. Johnson; nor so careful to maintain the ceremonies of life: and though he told Mr. Thrale once, that he had never sought to please till past thirty years old, considering the matter as hopeless, he had been always studious not to make enemies, by apparent preference of himself. It happened very comically, that the moment this curious conversation past, of which I was a silent auditress, was in the coach, in some distant province, either Shropshire or Derbyshire, I believe; and as soon as it was over, Mr. Johnson took out of his pocket a little book and read, while a gentleman of no small distinction for his birth and elegance, suddenly rode up to the carriage, and paying us all his proper compliments, was desirous not to neglect Dr. Johnson; but observing that he did not see him, tapt him gently on the shoulder—'Tis Mr. Ch—lm—ley, says my husband;—"Well, Sir! and what if it is Mr. Ch—lm—ley!" says the other sternly, just lifting his eyes a moment from his book, and returning to it again with renewed avidity.

He had sometimes fits of reading very violent; and when he was in earnest about getting through some particular pages, for I have heard him say he never read but one book, which he did not consider as obligatory, through in his whole life (and Lady Mary Wortley's Letters was the book); he would be quite lost to company, and withdraw all his attention to what he was reading, without the smallest knowledge or care about the noise made round him. His deafness made such conduct less odd and less difficult to him than it would have been to another man; but his advising others to take the same method, and pull a little book out when they were not entertained with what was going forward in society, seemed more likely to advance the growth of science than of polished manners, for which he always pretended extreme veneration.

Mr. Johnson indeed always measured other people's notions of every thing by his own, and nothing could persuade him to believe, that the

books which he disliked were agreeable to thousands, or that air and exercise which he despised
were beneficial to the health of other mortals. When
poor Smart, so well known for his wit and mis-
fortunes, was first obliged to be put in private
lodgings, a common friend of both lamented in
tender terms the necessity which had torn so
pleasing a companion from their acquaintance—
"A madman must be confined, Sir," (replies Dr.
Johnson;) but, says the other, I am now apprehen-
sive for his general health, he will lose the benefit
of exercise. "Exercise! (returns the Doctor) I
never heard that he used any: he might, for aught
I know, walk *to* the alehouse; but I believe he was
always *carried* home again."

It was however unlucky for those who delighted
to echo Johnson's sentiments, that he would not
endure from them to-day, what perhaps he had
yesterday, by his own manner of treating the subject, made them fond of repeating; and I fancy
Mr. B—— has not forgotten, that though his
friend one evening in a gay humour talked in
praise of wine as one of the blessings permitted
by heaven, when used with moderation, to lighten
the load of life, and give men strength to endure
it; yet, when in consequence of such talk *he*
thought fit to make a Bacchanalian discourse in
its favour, Mr. Johnson contradicted him somewhat roughly as I remember; and when to assure
himself of conquest he added these words, You

must allow me, Sir, at least that it produces truth; *in vino veritas*, you know, Sir—"That (replied Mr. Johnson) would be useless to a man who knew he was not a liar when he was sober."

When one talks of giving and taking the lie familiarly, it is impossible to forbear recollecting the transactions between the editor of Ossian and the author of the Journey to the Hebrides. It was most observable to me however, that Mr. Johnson never bore his antagonist the slightest degree of ill-will. He always kept those quarrels which belonged to him as a writer, separate from those which he had to do with as a man; but I never did hear him say in private one malicious word of a public enemy; and of Mr. Macpherson I once heard him speak respectfully, though his reply to the friend who asked him if *any man living* could have written such a book, is well known, and has been often repeated: "Yes, Sir; many men, many women, and many children."

I enquired of him myself if this story was authentic, and he said it was. I made the same enquiry concerning his account of the state of literature in Scotland, which was repeated up and down at one time by every body—"How knowledge was divided among the Scots, like bread in a besieged town, to every man a mouthful, to no man a bellyful." This story he likewise acknowledged, and said besides, "that some officious friend had carried it to Lord Bute, who only

answered—Well, well! never mind what he says—
he will have the pension all one."

Another famous reply to a Scotsman who commended the beauty and dignity of Glasgow, till
Mr. Johnson stopped him by observing, "that he
probably had never yet seen Brentford," was one
of the jokes he owned: and said himself, "that
when a gentleman of that country once mentioned
the lovely prospects common in his nation, he could
not help telling him, that the view of the London
road was the prospect in which every Scotsman
most naturally and most rationally delighted."

Mrs. Brooke received an answer not unlike this,
when expatiating on the accumulation of sublime
and beautiful objects, which form the fine prospect
UP the river St. Lawrence in North America;
"Come Madam (says Dr. Johnson), confess that
nothing ever equalled your pleasure in seeing that
sight reversed; and finding yourself looking at the
happy prospect DOWN the river St. Lawrence."
The truth is, he hated to hear about prospects and
views, and laying out ground and taste in gardening: "That was the best garden (he said) which
produced most roots and fruits; and that water
was most to be prized which contained most fish."
He used to laugh at Shenstone most unmercifully
for not caring whether there was any thing good
to *eat* in the streams he was so fond of, "as if (says
Johnson) one could fill one's belly with hearing
soft murmurs, or looking at rough cascades!"

He loved the sight of fine forest trees however, and detested Brighthelmstone Downs, "because it was a country so truly desolate (he said), that if one had a mind to hang one's self for desperation at being obliged to live there, it would be difficult to find a tree on which to fasten the rope." Walking in a wood when it rained, was, I think, the only rural image he pleased his fancy with; "for (says he) after one has gathered the apples in an orchard, one wishes them well baked, and removed to a London eating-house for enjoyment."

With such notions, who can wonder he passed his time uncomfortably enough with us, whom he often complained of for living so much in the country; "feeding the chickens (as he said I did) till I starved my own understanding. Get however (said he) a book about gardening, and study it hard, since you will pass your life with birds and flowers, and learn to raise the *largest* turnips, and to breed the *biggest* fowls." It was vain to assure him that the goodness of such dishes did not depend upon their size; he laughed at the people who covered their canals with foreign fowls, "when (says he) our own geese and ganders are twice as large: if we fetched better animals from distant nations, there might be some sense in the preference; but to get cows from Alderney, or waterfowl from China, only to see nature degenerating round one, is a poor ambition indeed."

Nor was Mr. Johnson more merciful with regard

to the amusements people are contented to call such: "You hunt in the morning (says he), and crowd to the public rooms at night, and call it *diversion*; when your heart knows it is perishing with poverty of pleasures, and your wits get blunted for want of some other mind to sharpen them upon. There is in this world no real delight (excepting those of sensuality), but exchange of ideas in conversation; and whoever has once experienced the full flow of London talk, when he retires to country friendships and rural sports, muſt either be contented to turn baby again and play with the rattle, or he will pine away like a great fish in a little pond, and die for want of his usual food."— "Books without the knowledge of life are useless (I have heard him say); for what should books teach but the art of *living?* To ſtudy manners however only in coffee-houses, is more than equally imperfeſt; the minds of men who acquire no solid learning, and only exiſt on the daily forage that they pick up by running about, and snatching what drops from their neighbours as ignorant as themselves, will never ferment into any knowledge valuable or durable; but like the light wines we drink in hot countries, please for the moment though incapable of keeping. In the ſtudy of mankind much will be found to swim as froth, and much muſt sink as feculence, before the wine can have its effeſt, and become that nobleſt liquor which rejoices the heart, and gives vigour to the imagination."

I am well aware that I do not, and cannot give each expression of Dr. Johnson with all its force or all its neatness; but I have done my beſt to record such of his maxims, and repeat such of his sentiments, as may give to those who knew him not, a juſt idea of his character and manner of thinking. To endeavour at adorning, or adding, or softening, or meliorating such anecdotes, by any tricks my inexperienced pen could play, would be weakness indeed; worse than the Frenchman who presides over the porcelain manufactory at Seve, to whom when some Greek vases were given him as models, he lamented *la triſteſſe de telles formes*; and endeavoured to assiſt them by cluſters of flowers, while flying Cupids served for the handles of urns originally intended to contain the ashes of the dead. The misery is, that I can recollect so few anecdotes, and that I have recorded no more axioms of a man whose every word merited attention, and whose every sentiment did honour to human nature. Remote from affectation as from error or falsehood, the comfort a reader has in looking over these papers, is the certainty that those were *really* the opinions of Johnson, which are related as such.

Fear of what others may think, is the great cause of affectation; and he was not likely to disguise his notions out of cowardice. He hated disguise, and nobody penetrated it so readily. I shewed him a letter written to a common friend, who was at some loss for the explanation of it: "Whoever wrote it (says our Doctor) could, if he chose it, make himself understood; but 'tis the letter of an *embarrassed man, Sir*;" and so the event proved it to be.

Mysteriousness in trifles offended him on every side: "it commonly ended in guilt (he said); for those who begin by concealment of innocent things, will soon have something to hide which they dare not bring to light." He therefore encouraged an openness of conduct, in women particularly, "who (he observed) were often led away when children, by their delight and power of surprising." He recommended, on something like the same principle, that when one person meant to serve another, he should not go about it slily, or as we say underhand, out of a false idea of delicacy, to surprise one's friend with an unexpected favour; "which, ten to one (says he), fails to oblige your acquaintance, who had some reasons against such a mode of obligation, which you might have known but for that superfluous cunning which you think an elegance. Oh! never be seduced by such silly pretences (continued he); if a wench wants a good gown, do not give her a fine smelling-bottle, because that is more delicate: as I once knew a lady lend the key of her library to a poor scribbling dependant, as if she took the woman for an ostrich that could digest iron." He said indeed, "that women were very difficult to be taught the proper manner of conferring pecuniary favours; that they always gave too much money or too little; for that they had an idea of delicacy accompanying their gifts, so that they generally rendered them either useless or ridiculous."

He did indeed say very contemptuous things of our sex; but was exceedingly angry when I told Miss Reynolds that he said, "It was well managed of some one to leave his affairs in the hands of his wife, because, in matters of business (said he), no woman ſtops at integrity." This was, I think, the only sentence I ever observed him solicitous to explain away after he had uttered it. He was not at all displeased at the recollection of a sarcasm thrown on a whole profession at once; when a gentleman leaving the company, somebody who sate next Dr. Johnson asked him, who he was? "I cannot exactly tell you Sir (replied he), and I would be loth to speak ill of any person who I do not know deserves it, but I am afraid he is an *attorney*." He did not however encourage general satire, and for the moſt part professed himself to feel directly contrary to Dr. Swift; "who (says he) hates the world, though he loves John and Robert, and certain individuals."

Johnson said always, "that the world was well conſtructed, but that the particular people disgraced the elegance and beauty of the general fabric." In the same manner I was relating once to him, how Dr. Collier observed, that the love one bore to children was from the anticipation one's mind made while one contemplated them: "We hope (says he) that they will some time make wise men, or amiable women; and we suffer 'em to take up our affection beforehand. One cannot love *lumps of flesh*, and little infants are nothing more. On the contrary (says Johnson), one can scarcely help wishing, while one fondles a baby, that it may never live to become a man; for it is *so* probable that when he becomes a man, he should be sure to end in a scoundrel." Girls were less displeasing to him; "for as their temptations were fewer (he said), their virtue in this life, and happiness in the next, were less improbable; and he loved (he said) to see a knot of little misses dearly."

Needle-work had a strenuous approver in Dr. Johnson, who said, "that one of the great felicities of female life, was the general consent of the world, that they might amuse themselves with petty occupations, which contributed to the lengthening their lives, and preserving their minds in a state of sanity." A man cannot hem a pocket-handkerchief (said a lady of quality to him one day), and so he runs mad, and torments his family and friends. The expression struck him exceedingly, and when one acquaintance grew troublesome, and another unhealthy, he used to quote Lady Frances's observation, "That a man cannot hem a pocket-handkerchief."

The nice people found no mercy from Mr. Johnson; such I mean as can dine only at four o'clock, who cannot bear to be waked at an unusual hour, or miss a stated meal without inconvenience. *He* had no such prejudices himself, and with difficulty forgave them in another. "Delicacy does not surely consist (says he) in impossibility to be pleased, and that is false dignity indeed which is content to depend upon others."

The saying of the old philosopher, who observes, That he who wants least is most like the gods, who want nothing; was a favourite sentence with Dr. Johnson, who on his own part required less attendance, sick or well, than ever I saw any human creature. Conversation was all he required to make him happy; and when he would have tea made at two o'clock in the morning, it was only that there might be a certainty of detaining his companions round him. On that principle it was that he preferred winter to summer, when the heat of the weather gave people an excuse to stroll about, and walk for pleasure in the shade, while he wished to sit still on a chair, and chat day after day, till somebody proposed a drive in the coach; and that was the most delicious moment of his life. "But the carriage must stop sometime (as he said), and the people would come home at last;" so his pleasure was of short duration.

I asked him why he doated on a coach so? and received for answer, "That in the first place, the company was shut in with him *there*; and could not escape, as out of a room: in the next place, he heard all that was said in a carriage, where it was my turn to be deaf:" and very impatient was he at my occasional difficulty of hearing. On this account he wished to travel all over the world; for the very act of going forward was delightful to him, and he gave himself no concern about accidents, which he said never happened: nor did the running-away of the horses on the edge of a precipice between Vernon and St. Denys in France convince him to the contrary; "for nothing came of it (he said), except that Mr. Thrale leaped out of the carriage into a chalk-pit, and then came up again, looking *as white!*" When the truth was, all their lives were saved by the greatest providence ever exerted in favour of three human creatures; and the part Mr. Thrale took from desperation was the likeliest thing in the world to produce broken limbs and death.

Fear was indeed a sensation to which Mr. Johnson was an utter stranger, excepting when some sudden apprehensions seized him that he was going to die; and even then he kept all his wits about him, to express the most humble and pathetic petitions to the Almighty: and when the first paralytic stroke took his speech from him, he instantly set about composing a prayer in Latin, at once to deprecate God's mercy, to satisfy himself that his mental powers remained unimpaired, and to keep them in exercise, that they might not perish by permitted stagnation. This was after we parted; but he wrote me an account of it, and I intend to publish that letter, with many more.

When one day he had at my house taken tincture of antimony instead of emetic wine, for a vomit, he was himself the person to direct us what to do for him, and managed with as much coolness and deliberation as if he had been prescribing for an indifferent person. Though on another occasion, when he had lamented in the most piercing terms his approaching dissolution, and conjured me solemnly to tell him what I thought, while Sir Richard Jebb was perpetually on the road to Streatham, and Mr. Johnson seemed to think himself neglected if the physician left him for an hour only, I made him a steady, but as I thought a very gentle harangue, in which I confirmed all that the Doctor had been saying, how no present danger could be expected; but that his age and continued ill health must naturally accelerate the arrival of that hour which can be escaped by none: "And this (says Johnson, rising in great anger) is the voice of female friendship I suppose, when the hand of the hangman would be softer."

Another day, when he was ill, and exceedingly low-spirited, and persuaded that death was not far distant, I appeared before him in a dark-coloured gown, which his bad sight, and worse apprehensions, made him mistake for an iron-grey. "Why do you delight (said he) thus to thicken the gloom of misery that surrounds me? is not here sufficient accumulation of horror without anticipated mourning?" This is not mourning Sir (said I), drawing the curtain, that the light might fall upon the silk, and shew it was a purple mixed with green. "Well, well (replied he, changing his voice), you little creatures should never wear those sort of clothes however; they are unsuitable in every way. What! have not all insects gay colours!" I relate these instances chiefly to shew that the fears of death itself could not suppress his wit, his sagacity, or his temptation to sudden resentment.

Mr. Johnson did not like that his friends should bring their manuscripts for him to read, and he liked still less to read them when they were brought: sometimes however when he could not refuse he would take the play or poem, or whatever it was, and give the people his opinion from some one page that he had peeped into. A gentleman carried him his tragedy, which, because he loved the author, Johnson took, and it lay about our rooms some time. What answer did you give your friend, Sir? said I, after the book had been called for. "I told him (replied he), that there was too much *Tig* and *Tirry* in it." Seeing me laugh most violently, "Why what would'st have, child?" (said he.) I looked at nothing but the dramatis, and there was *Tig*ranes and *Tiri*dates, or Teribazus, or such stuff. A man can tell but what he knows, and I never got any further than the first page. Alas, Madam! (continued he) how few books are there of which

one ever can possibly arrive at the *last* page! Was
there ever yet any thing written by mere man that
was wished longer by its readers, excepting Don
Quixote, Robinson Crusoe, and the Pilgrim's Progress?'' After Homer's Iliad, Mr. Johnson confessed that the work of Cervantes was the greatest
in the world, speaking of it I mean as a book of
entertainment; and when we consider that every
other author's admirers are confined to his country-
men, and perhaps to the literary classes among
them, while Don Quixote is a sort of common
property, an universal classic, equally tasted by the
court and the cottage, equally applauded in France
and England as in Spain, quoted by every servant,
the amusement of every age from infancy to de-
crepitude; the first book you see on every shelf, in
every shop, where books are sold, through all the
states of Italy; who can refuse his consent to an
avowal of the superiority of Cervantes to all other
modern writers? Shakespeare himself has, till
lately, been worshipped only at home, though his
plays are now the favourite amusements of Vienna;
and when I was at Padua some months ago, Romeo
and Juliet was acted there under the name of
Tragedia Veronese; while engravers and translators
live by the Hero of La Mancha in every nation,
and the sides of miserable inns all over England
and France, and I have heard Germany too, are
adorned with the exploits of Don Quixote. May
his celebrity procure my pardon for a digression in

praise of a writer who, through four volumes of the most exquisite pleasantry and genuine humour, has never been seduced to overstep the limits of propriety, has never called in the wretched auxiliaries of obscenity or profaneness; who trusts to nature and sentiment alone, and never misses of that applause which Voltaire and Sterne labour to produce, while honest merriment bestows her unfading crown upon Cervantes.

Dr. Johnson was a great reader of French literature, and delighted exceedingly in Boileau's works. Moliere I think he had hardly sufficient taste of; and he used to condemn me for preferring La Bruyere to the Duc de Rochefoucault, "who (he said) was the only *gentleman* writer who wrote like a professed author." The asperity of his harsh sentences, each of them a sentence of condemnation, used to disgust me however; though it must be owned, that, among the necessaries of human life, a *rasp* is reckoned one as well as a *razor*.

Mr. Johnson did not like any one who said they were happy, or who said any one else was so. "It is all *cant* (he would cry), the dog knows he is miserable all the time." A friend whom he loved exceedingly, told him on some occasion notwithstanding, that his wife's sister was *really* happy, and called upon the lady to confirm his assertion, which she did somewhat roundly as we say, and with an accent and manner capable of offending Mr. Johnson, if her position had not been sufficient, without any thing more, to put him in very ill humour. "If your sister-in-law is really the contented being she professes herself Sir (said he), her life gives the lie to every research of humanity; for she is happy without health, without beauty, without money, and without understanding." This story he told me himself; and when I expressed something of the horror I felt, "The same stupidity (said he) which prompted her to extol felicity she never felt, hindered her from feeling what shocks you on repetition. I tell you, the woman is ugly, and sickly, and foolish, and poor; and would it not make a man hang himself to hear such a creature say, it was happy?"

"The life of a sailor was also a continued scene of danger and exertion (he said); and the manner in which time was spent on shipboard would make all who saw a cabin envy a gaol." The roughness of the language used on board a man of war, where he passed a week on a visit to Capt. Knight, disgusted him terribly. He asked an officer what some place was called, and received for answer, that it was where the loplolly man kept his loplolly: a reply he considered, not unjustly, as disrespectful, gross, and ignorant; for though in the course of these Memoirs I have been led to mention Dr. Johnson's tenderness towards *poor* people, I do not wish to mislead my readers, and make them think he had any delight in *mean* manners or coarse expressions. Even dress itself, when it resembled that of the vulgar, offended him exceedingly; and when he had condemned me many times for not adorning my children with more show than I thought useful or elegant, I presented a little girl to him who came o'visiting one evening covered with shining ornaments, to see if he would approve of the appearance she made. When they were gone home, Well Sir, said I, how did you like little miss? I hope she was *fine* enough. "It was the finery of a beggar (said he), and you know it was; she looked like a native of Cow-lane dressed up to be carried to Bartholomew-fair."

His reprimand to another lady for crossing her little child's handkerchief before, and by that operation dragging down its head oddly and unintentionally, was on the same principle. "It is the beggar's fear of cold (said he) that prevails over such parents, and so they pull the poor thing's head down, and give it the look of a baby that plays about Westminster-Bridge, while the mother sits shivering in a *niche*."

I commended a young lady for her beauty and pretty behaviour one day however, to whom I thought no objections could have been made. "I saw her (says Dr. Johnson) take a pair of scissars in her left hand though; and for all her father is now become a nobleman, and as you say excessively rich, I should, were I a youth of quality ten years hence, hesitate between a girl so neglected, and a *negro*."

It was indeed aſtonishing how he *could* remark such minutenesses with a sight so miserably imperfeét; but no accidental position of a ribband escaped him, so nice was his observation, and so rigorous his demands of propriety. When I went with him to Litchfield and came down ſtairs to breakfaſt at the inn, my dress did not please him, and he made me alter it entirely before he would ſtir a ſtep with us about the town, saying moſt satirical things concerning the appearance I made in a riding-habit; and adding, "'Tis very ſtrange that such eyes as yours cannot discern propriety of dress: if I had a sight only half as good, I think I should see to the centre."

My compliances however were of little worth: what really surprised me was the viétory he gained over a Lady little accuſtomed to contradiétion, who had dressed herself for church at Streatham one Sunday morning, in a manner he did not approve, and to whom he said such sharp and pungent things concerning her hat, her gown, &c. that she haſtened to change them, and returning quite another figure received his applause, and thanked him for his reproofs, much to the amazement of her husband, who could scarcely believe his own ears.

Another lady, whose accomplishments he never denied, came to our house one day covered with diamonds, feathers, &c. and he did not seem inclined to chat with her as usual. I asked him why?

when the company was gone. "Why; her head looked so like that of a woman who shews puppets (said he), and her voice so confirmed the fancy, that I could not bear her to-day; when she wears a large cap, I can talk to her."

When the ladies wore lace trimmings to their clothes, he expressed his contempt of the reigning fashion in these terms: "A Brussels trimming is like bread sauce (said he), it takes away the glow of colour from the gown, and gives you nothing instead of it; but sauce was invented to heighten the flavour of our food, and trimming is an ornament to the manteau, or it is nothing. Learn (said he) that there is propriety or impropriety in every thing how slight soever, and get at the general principles of dress and of behaviour; if you then transgress them, you will at least know that they are not observed."

All these exactnesses in a man who was nothing less than exact himself, made him extremely impracticable as an inmate, though most instructive as a companion, and useful as a friend. Mr. Thrale too could sometimes over-rule his rigidity, by saying coldly, There, there, now we have had enough for one lecture, Dr. Johnson; we will not be upon education any more till after dinner, if you please —or some such speech: but when there was nobody to restrain his dislikes, it was extremely difficult to find any body with whom he could converse, without living always on the verge of a quarrel, or of something too like a quarrel to be pleasing. I came into the room, for example, one evening, where he and a gentleman, whose abilities we all respect exceedingly, were sitting; a lady who walked in two minutes before me had blown 'em both into a flame, by whispering something to Mr. S——d, which he endeavoured to explain away, so as not to affront the Doctor, whose suspicions were all alive. "And have a care, Sir (said he), just as I came in; the Old Lion will not bear to be tickled." The other was pale with rage, the Lady wept at the confusion she had caused, and I could only say with Lady Macbeth,

> Soh! you've displac'd the mirth, broke the good meeting
> With most admir'd disorder.

Such accidents however occurred too often, and I was forced to take advantage of my lost lawsuit, and plead inability of purse to remain longer in London or its vicinage. I had been crossed in my intentions of going abroad, and found it convenient, for every reason of health, peace, and pecuniary circumstances, to retire to Bath, where I knew Mr. Johnson would not follow me, and where I could for that reason command some little portion of time for my own use; a thing impossible while I remained at Streatham or at London, as my hours, carriage, and servants had long been at his command, who would not rise in the morning till twelve o'clock perhaps, and oblige me to make breakfast for him till the bell rung for dinner, though much displeased if the toilet was neglected, and though much of the time we passed together was spent in blaming or deriding, very justly, my neglect of œconomy, and waste of that money which might make many families happy. The original reason of our connection, his *particularly disordered health and spirits*, had been long at an end, and he had no other ailments than old age and general infirmity, which every professor of medicine was ardently zealous and generally attentive to palliate, and to contribute all in their power for the prolongation of a life so valuable. Veneration for his virtue, reverence for his talents, delight in his conversation, and habitual endurance of a yoke my husband first put upon me, and of which he contentedly bore his share for sixteen or seventeen years, made me go on so long with Mr. Johnson; but the perpetual confinement I will own to have been terrifying in the first years of our friendship, and irksome in the last; nor could I pretend to support it without help, when my coadjutor was no more. To the assistance we gave him, the shelter our house afforded to his uneasy fancies, and to the pains we took to sooth or repress them, the world perhaps is indebted for the three political pamphlets, the new edition and correction of his Dictionary, and for the Poets Lives, which he would scarce have lived, I think, and kept his faculties entire, to have written, had not incessant care been exerted at the time of his first coming to be our constant guest in the country; and several times after that, when he found himself particularly oppressed with diseases incident to the most vivid and fervent imaginations. I shall for ever consider it as the greatest honour which could be conferred on any one, to have been the confidential friend of Dr. Johnson's health; and to have in some measure, with Mr. Thrale's assistance, saved from distress at least, if not from worse, a mind great beyond the comprehension of common mortals, and good beyond all hope of imitation from perishable beings.

Many of our friends were earnest that he should write the lives of our famous prose authors; but he never made any answer that I can recollect to the proposal, excepting when Sir Richard Musgrave once was singularly warm about it, getting up and intreating him to set about the work immediately; he coldly replied, "*Sit down, Sir!*"

When Mr. Thrale built the new library at Streatham, and hung up over the books the portraits of his favourite friends, that of Dr. Johnson was last finished, and closed the number. It was almost impossible *not* to make verses on such an accidental combination of circumstances, so I made the following ones: but as a character written in verse will for the most part be found imperfect as a character, I have therefore written a prose one, with which I mean, not to complete, but to conclude these Anecdotes of the best and wisest man that ever came within the reach of my personal acquaintance, and I think I might venture to add, that of all or any of my readers:

Gigantic in knowledge, in virtue, in strength,
Our company closes with JOHNSON at length;
So the Greeks from the cavern of Polypheme past,
When wisest, and greatest, Ulysses came last.
To his comrades contemptuous, we see him look down,
On their wit and their worth with a general frown.
Since from Science' proud tree the rich fruit he receives,
Who could shake the whole trunk while they turn'd a few leaves.
His piety pure, his morality nice—
Protector of virtue, and terror of vice;
In these features Religion's firm champion display'd,
Shall make infidels fear for a modern crusade.
While th' inflammable temper, the positive tongue,
Too conscious of right for endurance of wrong,
We suffer from JOHNSON, contented to find,
That some notice we gain from so noble a mind;
And pardon our hurts, since so often we've found
The balm of instruction pour'd into the wound.
'Tis thus for its virtues the chemists extol
Pure rectified spirit, sublime alcohol;
From noxious putrescence, preservative pure,
A cordial in health, and in sickness a cure;
But expos'd to the sun, taking fire at his rays,
Burns bright to the bottom, and ends in a blaze.

It is usual, I know not why, when a character is given, to begin with a description of the person; that which contained the soul of Mr. Johnson deserves to be particularly described. His stature was remarkably high, and his limbs exceedingly large: his strength was more than common I believe, and his activity had been greater I have heard than such a form gave one reason to expect: his

features were strongly marked, and his countenance particularly rugged; though the original complexion had certainly been fair, a circumstance
somewhat unusual: his sight was near, and otherwise imperfect; yet his eyes, though of a light-grey
colour, were so wild, so piercing, and at times so
fierce, that fear was I believe the first emotion in
the hearts of all his beholders. His mind was so
comprehensive, that no language but that he used
could have expressed its contents; and so ponderous
was his language, that sentiments less lofty and
less solid than his were, would have been encum-
bered, not adorned by it.

Mr. Johnson was not intentionally however a
pompous converser; and though he was accused of
using big words as they are called, it was only
when little ones would not express his meaning
as clearly, or when perhaps the elevation of the
thought would have been disgraced by a dress less
superb. He used to say, "that the size of a man's
understanding might always be justly measured by
his mirth;" and his own was never contemptible.
He would laugh at a stroke of genuine humour, or
sudden sally of odd absurdity, as heartily and freely
as I ever yet saw any man; and though the jest
was often such as few felt besides himself, yet his
laugh was irresistible, and was observed immediately to produce that of the company, not merely
from the notion that it was proper to laugh when
he did, but purely out of want of power to forbear

it. He was no enemy to splendour of apparel or pomp of equipage—"Life (he would say) is barren enough surely with all her trappings; let us therefore be cautious how we ſtrip her." In matters of ſtill higher moment he once observed, when speaking on the subjeƈt of sudden innovation,—"He who plants a foreſt may doubtless cut down a hedge; yet I could wish methinks that even he would wait till he sees his young plants grow."

With regard to common occurrences, Mr. Johnson had, when I firſt knew him, looked on the ſtill-shifting scenes of life till he was weary; for as a mind slow in its own nature, or unenlivened by information, will contentedly read in the same book for twenty times perhaps, the very aƈt of reading it being more than half the business, and every period being at every reading better underſtood; while a mind more aƈtive or more skilful to comprehend its meaning is made sincerely sick at the second perusal; so a soul like his, acute to discern the truth, vigorous to embrace, and powerful to retain it, soon sees enough of the world's dull prospeƈt, which at firſt, like that of the sea, pleases by its extent, but soon, like that too, fatigues from its uniformity; a calm and a ſtorm being the only variations that the nature of either will admit.

Of Mr. Johnson's erudition the world has been the judge, and we who produce each a score of his sayings, as proofs of that wit which in him was inexhauſtible, resemble travellers who having visited

Delhi or Golconda, bring home each a handful of Oriental pearl to evince the riches of the Great Mogul. May the Public condescend to accept my *ill-strung* selection with patience at least, remembering only that they are relics of him who was great on all occasions, and, like a cube in architecture, you beheld him on each side, and his size still appeared undiminished.

As his purse was ever open to almsgiving, so was his heart tender to those who wanted relief, and his soul susceptible of gratitude, and of every kind impression; yet though he had refined his sensibility, he had not endangered his quiet, by encouraging in himself a solicitude about trifles, which he treated with the contempt they deserve.

It was well enough known before these sheets were published, that Mr. Johnson had a roughness in his manner which subdued the saucy, and terrified the meek: this was, when I knew him, the prominent part of a character which few durst venture to approach so nearly; and which was for that reason in many respects grossly and frequently mistaken; and it was perhaps peculiar to him, that the lofty consciousness of his own superiority, which animated his looks, and raised his voice in conversation, cast likewise an impenetrable veil over him when he said nothing. His talk therefore had commonly the complexion of arrogance, his silence of superciliousness. He was however seldom inclined to be silent when any moral or literary question was started: and it was on such occasions, that, like the sage in Rasselas, he spoke, and attention watched his lips; he reasoned, and conviction closed his periods: if poetry was talked of, his quotations were the readiest; and had he not been eminent for more solid and brilliant qualities, mankind would have united to extol his extraordinary memory. His manner of repeating deserves to be described, though at the same time it defeats all power of description; but whoever once heard him repeat an ode of Horace, would be long before they could endure to hear it repeated by another.

His equity in giving the character of living acquaintance ought not undoubtedly to be omitted in his own, whence partiality and prejudice were totally excluded, and truth alone presided in his tongue: a steadiness of conduct the more to be commended, as no man had stronger likings or aversions. His veracity was indeed, from the most trivial to the most solemn occasions, strict, even to severity; he scorned to embellish a story with fictitious circumstances, which (he used to say) took off from its real value. "A story (says Johnson) should be a specimen of life and manners; but if the surrounding circumstances are false, as it is no more a representation of reality, it is no longer worthy our attention."

For the rest—That beneficence which during his life increased the comforts of so many, may after his death be perhaps ungratefully forgotten;

but that piety which dictated the serious papers in the Rambler, will be for ever remembered; for ever, I think, revered. That ample repository of religious truth, moral wisdom, and accurate criticism, breathes indeed the genuine emanations of its great Author's mind, expressed too in a style so natural to him, and so much like his common mode of conversing, that I was myself but little astonished when he told me, that he had scarcely read over one of those inimitable essays before they went to the press.

I will add one or two peculiarities more, before I lay down my pen.——Though at an immeasurable distance from content in the contemplation of his own uncouth form and figure, he did not like another man much the less for being a coxcomb. I mentioned two friends who were particularly fond of looking at themselves in a glass—"They do not surprise me at all by so doing (said Johnson): they see, reflected in that glass, men who have risen from almost the lowest situations in life; one to enormous riches, the other to every thing this world can give—rank, fame, and fortune. They see likewise, men who have merited their advancement by the exertion and improvement of those talents which God had given them; and I see not why they should avoid the mirror."

The other singularity I promised to record, is this: That though a man of obscure birth himself, his partiality to people of family was visible on every occasion; his zeal for subordination warm even to bigotry; his hatred to innovation, and reverence for the old feudal times, apparent, whenever any possible manner of shewing them occurred. I have spoken of his piety, his charity, and his truth, the enlargement of his heart, and the delicacy of his sentiments; and when I search for shadow to my portrait, none can I find but what was formed by pride, differently modified as different occasions shewed it; yet never was pride so purified as Johnson's, at once from meanness and from vanity. The mind of this man was indeed expanded beyond the common limits of human nature, and stored with such variety of knowledge, that I used to think it resembled a royal pleasure-ground, where every plant, of every name and nation, flourished in the full perfection of their powers, and where, though lofty woods and falling cataracts first caught the eye, and fixed the earliest attention of beholders, yet neither the trim parterre nor the pleasing shrubbery, nor even the antiquated ever-greens, were denied a place in some fit corner of the happy valley.

THE END.

POSTSCRIPT.

Naples, Feb. 10, 1786.

SINCE the foregoing went to the press, having seen a passage from Mr. Boswell's Tour to the Hebrides, in which it is said, that *I could not get through Mrs. Montagu's Essay on Shakespeare*, I do not delay a moment to declare, that, on the contrary, I have always commended it myself, and heard it commended by every one else; and few things would give me more concern than to be thought incapable of tasting, or unwilling to testify my opinion of its excellence.

NOTES ON THE TEXT

The text of this reprint follows, in the main, that of the fourth edition. As will be seen from these notes, a collation of the first and fourth editions has revealed very few variations of importance. In some places it has been necessary to restore the reading of the first edition (pp. 56, 81, 102, 108, 169, 196) and occasionally I have made a correction or suggestion of my own (pp. 90, 105, 107, 133). Differences in punctuation and in the use of capital letters have not been recorded. The punctuation of the fourth edition is on the whole much more careful than that of the first.

p. 16, l. 8, *well as me* 1.

p. 20, l. 20, *Can you forbear* 1.

p. 46, l. 3, *Se acquien* 1.

p. 48, l. 2, *ou je nais, et ou je meurs* 1.

p. 53, l. 10, *forgot* 1.

p. 56, last line, *to add* 1; *to added* 4.

p. 65, l. 5 from bottom, *observations* 1.

p. 69, note l. 2, *cooks shops* 1.

p. 81, l. 5 from bottom, *I ever saw* 1; *I every saw* 4.

p. 90, l. 5 from bottom. Perhaps Mrs Piozzi wrote 'became.'

p. 93, last line, *n'appayez pas* 1.

p. 100, ll. 2, 3, *Clown's answer in As you like it* 1.

p. 102, l. 4, *than that which said he had* 1; *than that which he said had* 4. Hill conjectures the reading of the first edition to be what Mrs Piozzi meant to say.

p. 105, l. 15, *company, all that I could do* 1, 4.

p. 106, l. 10 from bottom, *tigurique* 1; *tugurique* 4.

p. 107, l. 4, *Skiæ* 1, 4, and so in Boswell's *Tour*. But Johnson wrote *Sciæ*, as appears from the facsimile of the MS. in Mr R. B. Adam's *Catalogue*.

p. 108, l. 13 from bottom, *perderebbe* 1; *perderebbi* 4. Mrs Piozzi's mistakes in Italian (*se* for *si*; *conquesto* for *con questo*), to which my attention was called by Mr E.

Bullough, have been left in the text. See Birkbeck Hill, *Johnsonian Miscellanies* 1, 261, 262.

p. 123, ll. 13, 14, *recovering disorders* 1, 4; *recovering [from] disorders* (Hill).

p. 127, l. 1 of verse, *prey in [on] vice* (Hill).

p. 133, l. 8 from bottom. The emendation 'on end' is tempting, but Johnson describes 'an end' as probably corrupted from 'on end.'

p. 134, l. 7, *for ought I see* 1.

p. 144, l. 11, *sudden* 1.

p. 151, l. 11, *Aligu* 1.

p. 153, l. 3. Hill prints [*sic*] after 'were.'

p. 161, last line, *and does nothing* 1, 4; *and [who] does nothing* (Hill).

p. 169, l. 13, *Mrs. Brooke* 1; *Mrs. Brook* 4.

p. 170, l. 13, *who he often complained of* 1.

p. 182, l. 17, *spent shipboard* 1.

p. 196 (Postscript), l. 3, *Hebrides* 1; *Hedrides* 4.

INDEX

For EU product safety concerns, contact us at Calle de José Abascal, 56–1°, 28003 Madrid, Spain or eugpsr@cambridge.org.

www.ingramcontent.com/pod-product-compliance
Ingram Content Group UK Ltd.
Pitfield, Milton Keynes, MK11 3LW, UK
UKHW012328130625
459647UK00009B/143